W.H. Strobridge

Catalogue of a private collection of ancient coins

W.H. Strobridge

Catalogue of a private collection of ancient coins

ISBN/EAN: 9783741139680

Manufactured in Europe, USA, Canada, Australia, Japa

Cover: Foto ©ninafisch / pixelio.de

Manufactured and distributed by brebook publishing software (www.brebook.com)

W.H. Strobridge

Catalogue of a private collection of ancient coins

Catalogue

OF A

PRIVATE COLLECTION

OF

Ancient Coins,

AND AT THE CLOSE

A FEW MODERN COINS,

WITH AN ADDENDA.

TO BE SOLD BY AUCTION

AT

CLINTON HALL, ASTOR PLACE,

ON THE AFTERNOONS OF

Tuesday, Wednesday, Thursday and Friday,

OCTOBER 6th, 7th, 8th and 9th,

COMMENCING EACH DAY AT THREE O'CLOCK.

The Messrs. LEAVITT, Auctioneers.

CATALOGUE BY WM. H. STROBRIDGE.

INTRODUCTION.

ᵒᵁᴳᴴ this collection of ancient coins deserves a better fate than to be broken up, there is still much to reconcile us to its destiny, in the consideration that its materials will greatly promote the growth of other collections, and thereby advance the interests of numismatic science amongst us.

It is by studying such a collection as this that the importance of this kind of learning is understood; for it is almost alone in such a field that any satisfactory information concerning the religion, the civilization, and social life of ancient races can be acquired.

Count Scipio Maffei, of Verona, during the early part of the last century, in "A Comparison of the Use of Inscriptions and Medals," calls these two sorts of monuments "the eyes of learning;" certain it is that it is through these eyes we must look if we would see the buried nations as they appeared when acting their proper parts on the stage of life.

Vanity or prejudice may have influenced the historian, and given a false coloring to his pages, but the record that we find inscribed upon a coin may be safely taken for a fact. In this I do not include symbolical representations, which are almost as common among the moderns as the ancients. We miss the majestic form of Jupiter Aetophorus on modern coins, but the Olympian bird, holding the thunder in his talons, has been retained. Not in Jupiter, but "in God we trust." Some of the cumbrous machinery of paganism has been abolished, but the goddess of Liberty still holds her place; and Fame sounds her trumpet, and Vic- the conquering days of Alexander and

t coins is in the pictures which they give mber of facts which they contain.

how the great men and women of antiuity looked; and, if we would see true and undoubted representa- tins of their altars and temples, their bridges and ships, their galleys w.h tier upon tier of oars, their gladiators and the vast amphitheatres in wich they fought, the courses on which their chariot races were won, wth the frightened horses dashing madly past the image of Taxaxip- pṣ—in short, if we would see illustrations of public and private life, as

INTRODUCTION.

it existed in the distant past, we can look for them nowhere but on coins.

In making up this catalogue, I have occasionally introduced such notes as occurred to me at the time of writing, believing that I would be thanked by some, and pardoned by the rest, of my readers for so doing. And I hope that its reception will be such as to encourage others, with more leisure and greater ability, to indulge in similar but more extensive illustrations.

It remains for me only to add to what I have advanced concerning the study of ancient coins, a few words of hearty and richly-merited commendation of this particular collection.

It has been formed with enthusiasm, as well as with learning and judgment, and I am sensible that it would be difficult to speak the full truth in its favor, and at the same time preserve the appearance of candor and moderation.

It will perhaps be sufficient for me to say that a large proportion of the coins are exceptionally fine, and that many of them are so rare, that, in despair of originals, we have heretofore been satisfied to possess British Museum copies.

Purchasers at this sale may rest assured of the genuineness of their coins, and no reasonable pains have been spared to make the attribution and description accurate.

A few good modern coins and medals will be found at the close of the catalogue, and in the addenda.

WM. H. STROBRIDGE.

CLINTON HALL, Sept. 15, 1874.

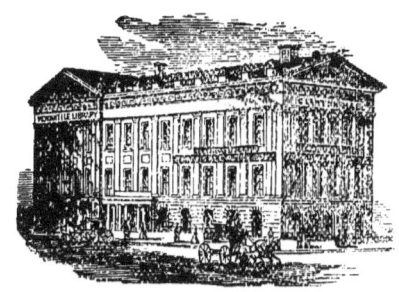

CATALOGUE.

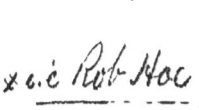

GREEK COINS.

1 ÆGINA, *Attica.* First coinage. A sea tortoise in high relief; rev. *four* deep punch marks. Didrachm.
2 ——— Another with ornamented border on shell, back smooth; rev. punch mark in *five* compartments.
3 ——— Didrachm of improved design; shell covered with knobs; rev. as before, distinguished as the land tortoise.
4 ——— Diobolus (with AIΔ), obolus, and half obolus; very rare. 3 pieces
5 ——— Obolus, ridge dividing shell, *sunk;* rev. incusum in the form of an Egyptian cross.
6 ARGOS, *Argolis.* Three dolphins A., rev. hollow with five compartments. C. size 8.
7 ——— Two dolphins A., rev. like last. C. size 8
8 ——— Two dolphins and tripod; rev. head, A. C. size 10
9 ——— Head of Juno with crown, A P Γ inscribed thereon; rev. Pallas striking l. with lance. Ex. fine and rare (sage green). C. size 12
10 ATHENS, *Attica.* Helmeted head of Minerva to r.; rev. owl in hollow square, spray of olive above, AΘE., Tet. Size 13

[This and the following tetradrachms, to Nos. 16 and 17, were prior to the time of Phidias and Pericles. The Abbe Barthelemy says that the Griffon which appears on the casque of Minerva at a later period, was copied from the one on the celebrated statue of this goddess by Phidias. Nos. 16 and 17 are examples. So perfect is the preservation of these coins, that it is doubtful if the seven tetradrachms in this collection have lost as many grains in weight.]

Greek Coins.

11 ATHENS, *Attica.* Head of Minerva to r., olive branch on helmet ; rev. as before. Deeper indentation. Tet. Size 14

12 —— Another tetradrachm of the clump form, high relief on both sides, no indentation. Size 12

13 —— Tetradrachm with the owl much smaller than on other examples; altogether very rude.

14 —— Another, owl very large.

15 —— Drachma, half do. (triobolus) ; third do. (diobolus), obolus and half obolus ; all of the early form, with indented reverses. 5 pieces

16 —— Helmeted head of Pallas, in beaded circle ; rev. owl on diota ; to l. grasshopper : ΑΘΕ ΛΥΣΑΝ-ΓΛΑΥ-ΚΟΣ-ΑΘΗΝ-ΒΙ-ΣΩ, tetradrachm of the age of Pericles and Phidias, (the 5th Cent. before our era). Size 19

17 —— Helmeted head of Pallas r., earrings and necklace ; rev. owl on diota ΑΘΕ ΔΗΙΕ* ΜΗΡΩ ΜΗ, all within olive wreath. Tet. Size 21

18 —— Helmeted head. 8 pointed star on casque ; rev. owl with raised wings on olive branch, ΑΘΗΝΑ above, and ΚΗΡΑΜ below. Similar obv. ; rev. Jupiter launching thunderbolt, to r. owl. Similar obv.; rev. Jupiter as before, to l. olive tree, ΑΘΕ ; obv. as before, rev. two owls face to face, ΑΘΕ ; obv. bust of Pallas to the waist, rev. owl. C. size 7 to 12, in fair condition. Very rare lot. 5 pieces

19 ELEUSIS, *Attica.* Female seated on shield ; rev. Sow to r. ; above, two ears of wheat. Well preserved and *very rare.* C. size 10

20 CORINTH, *Achaia.* Helmeted head of Pallas to l. ; to r., cuirass, ΑΛ ; rev. Pegasus to l., below the Phœnician Koph. (See Humphrey, p. 24.) Didrachm oblong in shape and of remarkable breadth. 14x17. Extremely rare.

21 —— Helmeted head of Pallas, l. to r. torch ; rev. as before. Didrachm.

22 —— Helmeted head of Pallas to r. above Λ ; rev. Pegasus to r. Didrachm.

23 —— Head of Pallas, full face ; rev. Pegasus. Very rare. S. obolus.

Greek Coins.

24 CORINTH. Head filleted to l. ; rev Jupiter hurling thunderbolt, to r. Cornucopiæ, below K ; obv. Pegasus, rev. trident ; obv. Pegasus, rev. horseman. C., well preserved and rare.
3 pieces

25 SICYON, *Achiae*. Bird flying to l., ΣE ; rev. bird flying, in olive wreath. Drachma.

26 —— Pegasus (walking) to l., ΣI ; rev. Pegasus flying. S. diobolus. Rare.

27 —— Bird flying to r. above ΣI ; rev. tripod in a wreath ; obv. female head to r., rev. bird with raised wings, ΣI. C. Fair preservation. 2 pieces

28 ELIS. Eagle with hare in his talons flying to r. ; rev. winged thunderbolt in sunken square FA. Extremely fine. Drachma.

NOTE.—This coin, according to Humphrey, was formerly attributed to Faleria in Etruria. See this author on coins of Elis.

29 THEBES, *Boeotia*. Buckler ; rev. Diota ΘES, oval incusum : of beautiful work, as it came from the die. Tridrachm.

30 —— Boeotian Shield ; rev. vase, above, club, Θ ; Hemidrachm.

31 ISMENE, *Boeotia*. Veiled head of Ceres to l., rev. goat standing to l., ΙΣΜΗΝ. Beautiful and rare. Tridrachm.
Size 18

32 BOEOTIA. Buckler ; rev. Diota ΑΓΛΑ. Tridrachm, pierced.

33 —— Full face of Minerva ; rev. Neptune standing, resting on his trident, BOI ; Turreted head, full face ; rev. Eagle with spread wings. Buckler ; rev. Trident and others, C. In ordinary condition. 5 pieces

34 HISTIAEA, *Euboea*. Woman's head crowned with grapes and vines; earrings and necklace ; rev. Draped female figure on prow, ΙΣΤΙΑΙΕΩΝ. Drachma.

35 —— Same ; rev. *Naked* female on prow. Drachm.

36 ERETRIA (or Erythrae), *Euboea*. Head of a bacchante ; rev. Bull about to lie down. C. Ordinary. Rare.

37 CHALCIS, *Euboea*. Female head to r. ; rev. Eagle devouring a serpent. Fair condition. Drachma.

38 PHOCIS. Head of a young man, in beaded circle, ΦΩ ; rev. Bull's head, front view, in laurel wreath. Drachma.

39 —— Bull's head, front view, in high relief, ΦΩ ; rev. Boar's head in a hollow square. S. (Diobolus.)

8 *Greek Coins.*

40 PHOCIS. Head of Ceres; rev. Fore part of a boar. Fine.
C. Size 6

41 DELPHI, *Phocis.* Veiled head of Apollo, or according to Eckhel, of the Sybil Herophila to l.; rev. Apollo holding a branch of laurel, sitting on the cortina before a tripod, his left arm resting on his lyre, ΑΜΦΙΚΤΙΟ. In surprising preservation and very rare. Tetradrachm.

42 LOCRIS, *Opuntii.* Head of Proserpine, with earrings and necklace of pearls; rev. Ajax charging, to r. ΟΠΟΝΤΙΩΝ, in the field a bunch of grapes. Equal to last. Tetradrachm.

43 —— Another of the same type. Drachma, pierced.

44 LETE, *Macedonia.* Pan carrying off a nymph; rev. Square punch-mark in four divisions. Pierced, large tridrachm.
Size 18

45 —— Drachma of the same type, ΛE (from right to left), as rudely formed.

46 —— Another of the rudest possible work. Very rare.

47 NEAPOLIS, *Macedonia.* Mask front; rev. Punch-mark, ancient counterfeit. Didrachm. Very rare.

48 —— Woman's head to r.; rev. Mask. Pierced, drachm.

49 AMPHIPOLIS, *Macedonia.* Nearly full face of Apollo in high relief; rev. Torch and tripod in a sunken square, around, ΑΜΦΙΠΟΛΙΤΕΩΝ in a second square. Tet. of extreme beauty and rarity.

50 MACEDONIA, 1*st Province.* Head of Diana with bow and quiver, in a beaded circle, embossed Macedonian shield; rev. ΜΑΚΕΔΟΝΩΝ ΝΡΩΤΗΣ, three monograms and club, all within wreath of oak leaves; in exergue thunderbolt. Pierced, yet a very beautiful tetradrachm. Size 19

51 —— A variation of same type, different ornaments on shield, and without monograms on rev. Size 20

52 —— Bare head of female, with flowing hair; rev. Club between altar and tripod, AESILLAS (Latin letters); all within laurel wreath. Tet. Size 20

53 LAMIA, *Thessaly.* Laureated head of Apollo; rev. Punchmarks in 4 compartments. Small thick coin (half aureus). Gold. Extremely fine and rare.

Greek Coins. 9

54 LARISSA, *Thessaly.* In a circle of dots, female head with earrings to l.; rev. Bridled horse galloping to r., ΛΑΡΙΣΑ. Didrachm.

55 —— Full face of Medusa, or (following Pembroke) of the fountain Hyperia personified; rev. Horse about to lie down. ΛΑΡΙΣΑΙΩΝ. Didrachm.

56 —— Man holding a bull by the horns, both running to l.; rev. Bridled horse galloping to r., ΛΑΡΙΣΑΙΑ; all in hollow. Didrachm.

57 —— Same type. Man and bull running to r. and horse to l. Didrachm.

NOTE.—These coins of Thessaly are highly illustrative of the allusions to be found in Homer to the horsemanship of Achilles, who was lord of this country, and renowned beyond the rest of the Greeks of his time for horse and chariot racing. They are of most excellent workmanship, and in superb preservation.

58 COSSEA, *Thrace.* Figure in the Roman habit, accompanied by lictors carrying rods, the three walking to l., in exergue ΚΟΣΩΝ; rev. Eagle holding in right talons a laurel crown. A coin of Marcus Junius Brutus. Very beautiful and rare. Gold. Size 13

59 MARONEA, *Thrace.* (Founded by Maron, son of Bacchus.) Female head crowned with a vine; rev. Nude figure standing, holding a bunch of grapes, ΔΙΟΝΥΣΟΣ ΣΩΤΗΡΟΣ ΜΑΡΩΝΙΤΩΝ. As it came from the die. C. Size 17

60 —— A variation of the same tye, and nearly a duplicate.

61 —— Bunch of grapes; rev. Punch-mark, small billon.

62 SESTUS, *Chersonesus Thracia.* Female head to l.; rev. Nude female seated, l. ΣΗΣΤΙΝΩΝ. C. Ex. rare. Size 14

63 ABDERA, *Thrace.* Head of Apollo in a square, name of the city around; rev. Griffon lying down, to l. Drachm. Extremely rare. In fair preservation.

64 CARDIA, *Chersonesus Thracia.* Lion's head, open mouth to l.; rev. in hollow, flower of the pomegranate. Drachma.

65 —— Obv. as before; rev. (in a square) a vase. Drachma.

66 —— Figure standing; rev. Lion looking back. Perfectly patinated. Dark green, rare. C. Size 10

67 ISTRUS, *Mœsia.* Double head, two female faces nearly full, up and down; rev. eagle with a fish in his tallons ΙΣΤΡΙΗ; below, A. Extremely rare. Drachma.

Greek Coins.

68 OLBIOPOLIS, *Sarmatia.* Bearded head of Pan; rev. bow, quiver and axe. OΛBIO. Very rare. C. Size 14

69 PANTICAPAEUM, *Chersonesus-Tauricus.* Bearded head of Pan; rev. cornucopia between the caps and stars of the Dioscuri. NANTI. Very rare. C. Size 10

70 DYRRHACHIUM, *Illyricum.* Cow suckling calf to r., head turned to left; rev. plan of the garden of Alcinöus, around ΔΥΡ and club; large didrachm. Very rare. Size 14

71 —— Cow suckling calf to l., head to r.; rev. as before. Didrachm.

72 —— Cow suckling calf, above ΜΕΝΙΣΚΟΣ; rev. garden of Alcinous, around ΔΥΡ. ΑΥ. ΙΣ. ΚΟΥ. Drachm.

73 THASUS, *Island.* Female ? head crowned with ivy; rev. Hercules standing to l., ΗΡΑΚΛΕΣ ΣΩΤΗΡΟΞ, ΘΑΣΙΩΝ. Tet. Size 20

74 —— Head to l.; rev. club, ΘΑΣΙΩΝ within wreath of laurel. Pierced, drachma. Very rare.

75 —— Pan on one knee to r.; rev. punch marks. Drachma.

76 LYTHUS, *Crete.* Eagle flying to l.; rev. boar's head in a hollow square, ΥΤΤΕΘΝ. Didrachm. Large size.

77 POLYRHENIUM, *Crete.* Woman's head, earrings, to l.; rev. bull's head, front face, in hollow. Drachm. Rare.

78 GORTYNA, *Crete.* Ox standing to l., head to r.; rev. Polypus in a hollow square. Pierced, drachma.

79 CHIOS, *Island.* Sphinx to l., in the field diota and cluster of grapes; rev. open cross, four squares grained, ΙΛΛΜΓΝΟΣ Didrachm.

80 —— Spinx seated, to l. vase; rev. hollow in four compartments. Drachm.

81 —— Two small coins in copper and lead. Rare.

82 CALYMNA, *Island.* Head of a warrior to right, with helmet protecting the *face*; rev. five stringed lyre and ΚΑΛΥΜΝΙΟΝ in a beaded square. Extremely rare, large didrachm. Size 14

83 SAMOS. Lion's head, front face, ΣΑ; rev. young Hercules on his knees strangling serpents, ΣΥΝ. Fine and rare. Tetradrachm.

84 —— Laureated head of Apollo to r.; rev. lion's face. Pierced, but well patinated and fine. C.

Greek Coins.

85 Cos, *Island.* Laureated head of Apollo; rev. lyre *KΩIΩN EMMEN* within wreath. Very fine and rare. C. Size 16

86 Rhodes, *Island.* Full face of Apollo, radiated head; rev. flower and bud of the rose, below Po, to l. woman standing, *MNAΣIMAXOΣ*, all in beaded circle. Large didrachm.

87 —— Nearly full face of Apollo; rev. rose, below PO, above *PIΣTOBIOΣ* in hollow. Didrachm.

88 —— Radiated head of Apollo r.; rev. rose in a sunken square P O., above *TANHΣ.* Very sharp, rare variety. S. Size 10

89 —— Head radiated, full face ; rev. rose and thunderbolt in incusum. Hemi-drachm.

90 —— Head of Apollo on full-blown rose ; rev. full length figure of Victory, with different inscriptions. C. Size 12. 3 pieces

91 —— Radiated head of Apollo, full face ; rev. *Lily* and others. C. 3 pieces

NOTE.—The head of Apollo, on the coin of Rhodes, is acknowledged to be among the finest examples of Greek genius. Certainly nothing can be more superb than the didrachms in this series.

92 Seriphus (perhaps Sicyone in Achaia). Chimera to l., *ΣI*; rev. bird flying. Drachma.

93 —— Same type. Half drachma.

94 Siphnus. Bird flying; rev. *ΣI* in wreath. C. 3 varieties.

95 Eresus, *Lesbos.* Beautiful female head (Sappho?) to l.; rev. E club P, within wreath formed of stalks of wheat. Excessively rare. C. Size 10

96 Sardis, *Lydia.* Head of Hercules r. ; rev. club, *ΣAPΔIA-NON* and monogram within wreath. C. Size 10

97 Cnidus, *Doris.* Star of 16 points ; rev. diota, *KPO.* S. Hemi-drachm.

98 —— Lion's head, front face ; rev. star of 16 points. S. Obolus.

99 Cyrene, *Cyrenaica.* Head of Jupiter Ammon in beaded circle within hollow square, *KΓPA* (for Cyrene) in corners; rev. the sacred silphium plant. Beautiful and rare. Drachm.

100 Barce, *Cyrenaica.* Obv. Head of Jupiter Ammon; rev. the silphium plant. Drachm.

Greek Coins.

101 ARADUS, *Phœnicia*. Turreted head of Cybele to r.; rev. Victory walking l., APAΔIΩN - ΓMPAO within laurel wreath. Tetradrachm. Extremely fine and rare.

102 —— Bee within beaded circle; rev. standing before a palm tree, a stag, APAΔIΩN. Beautiful work. Drachm.

103 —— Radiated head of Apollo to r.; rev. two ears of barley and branch of grape vine, APAΔIΩN. Fair preservation. C.
                   Size 12

104 EPHESUS, *Ionia*. Bee, $E\Phi$; rev. fore part of stag, to l. palm tree, OPXAMENIOΣ. Fine and rare. Tetradrachm.

105 —— Diademed head of woman to r.; rev. bee, $E\Phi$. Thick copper coin, very fine and rare.   Size 12

NOTE.—It is related that when the founders of Ephesus set out on their expedition, the muses, in the form of bees, flew before them, directing their course.

106 ERYTHREA, *Ionia*. Head of Hercules in lion-skin coif; rev. bow, quiver and club, to r. Cithera, to l. owl, EPΓ-ANEΛΛAE. As it came from the die. Drachm.

107 SMYRNA, *Ionia*. Laureated female head in beaded circle; rev. woman seated, in the field a star of eight points, ΣMYPN-AIΩN. Rare. Thick.   C. size 15

108 TEOS, *Ionia*. Griffon and dolphin; rev. punch marks in four compartments. Small silver coin. Rare.
    (Similar to coins of Abdera.)

109 —— Head of Pallas to l.; rev. Griffon to l. Copper. Rare

110 SIDE, *Pamphilia*. Helmeted head of Mars to r.; rev. Victory, holding a wreath in right hand, passing to l., ΔE, and fruit of the pomegranate pierced by arrow in field. Tetradrachm.

111 —— Head of Mars counter-marked with a full face of Apollo on neck; rev. Victory and pomegranate, ΣIΔH. Light green patination. C. Fine and rare.

NOTE.—Side was intimately connected with Aradus in Phoenicies, of which, perhaps this counter-mark was a token, Apollo being much patronized at Aradus.

112 SELGE, *Pisidia*. Within a beaded circle two athletes, wrestling; rev. a slinger hurling a stone; in the field, triguetra, EΣTFEΔ IVS, all in hollow square. Very interesting and rare. Large tridrachm.   Size 16

Greek Coins. 13

113 SELGE, *Pisidia*. Two wrestlers as before, E between; rev. slinger throwing a stone, between his legs Q, to r. triquetra and club, legend as before. Fine and rare.
                          Didrachm.

114 SINOPE, *Paphalonia*. Within beaded circle female head, with necklace and earrings, front face; rev. eagle, wings spread, ΣΙΝΩ. Extremely fine and rare.   S. size 8

115 —— Woman's head, front; rev. quiver and bow—NΩΠ.
                          C. size 10

116 APAMEA, *Phrygia*. Serpents entwined, between them star of 8 points and other mystic symbols, to r. thyrsus wtth serpent twining, ΑΠ; rev. within a ring formed of clusters of grapes, the mystic chest consecrated to the worship of Bacchus. Tetradrachm.

117 ANCYRA, *Phrygia*. Woman's head, front face (perhaps mask); rev. anchor, to r. beetle, to l. ΑΝΩ. Hemidrachm. Rare.

118 ABYDOS, *Troas*. Front face or mask; rev. punch mark in 10 compartments. Very early coin, nearly as old as those of Ægina. Rare. Drachm.

119 —— Mask, Gorgon face; rev. anchor. Drachm.

120 ILIUM, *Troas*. Man's head bare to r.; rev. Pallas standing, ΙΛΙ. A beautiful little coin, perfectly patinated.   C.

121 —— Laureated head to r.; rev. half-length figure of Pallas to l. Beautiful and rare.   C. size 10

122 —— Helmeted head of Pallas to r.; rev. Pallas standing l. And another.   2 pieces

123 ALEXANDRIA, *Troas*. Turreted head of Cybele to r., in Latin letters COL TRO; rev. Roman eagle, on standard COA TRO. Patinated.   C. size 14

124 SIGEUM, *Troas*. Head of Pallas, nearly full face; rev. owl. Small coppers. Patinated.   3 pieces

125 CAETHEA, *Cea*. Laureated head of Apollo to r.; rev. bunch of grapes; to l. star of 8 points, ΚΑΡΘ. Patinated. Fine and rare.   C. Size 12

126 —— Obv. as above; rev. bunch of grapes and bee; another, similar obv.; rev. fore part of an animal surrounded by rays; one with head and rays on both sides, and one with woman's head; rev. bee in wreath. Rare lot.   C. 4 pieces

127 DARDANUS. Head to r.; rev. fore part of a sheep or goat surrounded by rays. Small copper.

128 JULIS (or CORESIA), *Cea*. Head of Jupiter to r.; rev. bee; rev. star of 5 points, uncertain letters between the points. Rare copper coins. Well patinated. 2 pieces

129 MASSILIA. Head of Bacchus; rev. lion with open mouth walking to r., ΜΑΣΣ. Drachm. 2 pieces

130 —— Head of Venus to l.; rev. bull, ΜΑΣΣ. Fine. C.

131 PHŒNICIA. Head of Jupiter; rev. bow, arrow and club, and line of Phœnician characters; and another; drachm and smaller. Very fine coins. 2 pieces

132 INCERTA. Head to r.; rev. in hollow square two rams' heads. Small coin, in fine condition. Gold.

133 —— Head laureated of a woman; rev. harp. 3 drachma

134 —— Ram standing, below Janus head = head, rev. two Goats butting = head, rev. boar's head = head, rev. bull's head, front face = head; rev. fore part of a boar. C. 5 pieces

135 —— Another lot, equally uncertain. C. 7 pieces

136 PERSIA. Struck by Darius, son of Hystaspes, about 520 years B.C. Man on one knee discharging an arrow from bow, quiver at his back; rev. deep punch mark. An excellent example. S. Drachma.

137 —— Similar. Showing the figure more nearly at full length, also with a spear slung across his shoulder. In equally good preservation. Drachm.

[These coins are better known as "darics," although that term is also applied to the gold coins of Darius.]

INCUSED COINAGE OF MAGNA GRÆCIA.

138 SYBARIS, *Lucania* (destroyed B.C., Anno 510). Bull looking back, in exergue ΥΜ.—the first two letters of the name of the city if read from r. to l. the Σ being placed face downwards. Fine and extremely rare. Drachma.

139 CROTONA, *Bruttium*. A tripod; rev. tripod incused (a variation of obverse). Remarkable and fine didrachm.

140 METAPONTUM, *Lucania*. Ear of wheat or barley, META within a beaded circle, also two plain rings within and without the same; rev. incused, the ring, a circle of short rays. Very fine and rare didrachm.

141 —— Of the same age and type, MET. Drachma. Extremely fine.

142 CAULONIA, *Bruttium* (500 years before our era). A naked figure holding a branch in one hand, and in the other a small figure with two branches, to r. a stag, ΟΛΥΑΚ, which read from r. to l. is Kaulo; rev. incused. Large didrachm. Size 17

143 POSIDONIA (the modern Pæstum). Neptune striking r., in the field a stag, legend to l. (faint); rev. incused. Very early. Didrachm. Rare.

AUTONOMOUS COINS OF THE CITIES OF MAGA GRÆCIA.

CAMPANIA.

144 NEAPOLIS. Head of Parthenopeia (ancient home of the city) with necklace and earrings to r.; ΑΡΤΕΩΝ and Victory in the field; rev. Victory crowning bull with a human face, (Bacchus represented in this form), ΝΕΑΠΟΛΙΤΩΝ in exergue. Rare variety. Didrachm.

145 —— Head of Parthenopeia to l., earrings and necklace, hair in a net, behind head diota; rev. as before. Didrachm.

146 —— Head to l., behind, elephant; rev. as before, BI under the bull; in hollow. Didrachm.

NOTE.—Parthenopeia was a Siren famed for her beauty, whose singing, if Ovid tells the truth:
"Oft had drowned among the neighb'ring seas,
The list'ning wreath and made destruction please."

147 —— Head to l., bandeau, necklace and earrings; rev. Victory crowning bull to l., ΛΟΥ under the bull, in exergue ΝΕΟΠ-ΟΛΙΤΟΝ. Extremely fine. Didrachm.

148 —— Head of Parthenopeia to l. in beaded circle, necklace and earrings, and hair in net; to r. mask; rev, in hollow, Victory crowning human-headed bull. Didrachm.

16   *Greek Coins.*

149 NEAPOLIS. Head of Venus crowned with a wreath of roses to r., in field Apex (cap of a flamen); rev. Victory, etc., to r.; Didrachm.
150 —— Head of Parthenopeia to r., necklace and earrings, hair in net; in the field club; rev. as before, club and O between legs. Didrachm.
151 —— Head of Arethusa to r., to r. two dolphins; rev as before. Didrachm.
152 —— Head of Ceres veiled to r.; rev. tripod. Half stater, electrum.
153 —— Laureated head of Apollo to r.; rev. horse standing; between his legs * - NEAΠOΛITON.   C. size 13
154 —— Same head to l.; rev. tripod; another, fore part of the Minotaur (as on coins of Gelas); a third, similar to the didrachms, and two others. All beautifully patinated and rare varieties. Smaller than last.   C. 5 pieces
155 —— Didrachms of good quality, but inferior to preceding.
2 pieces
156 —— Similar lot.   2 "
157 —— Copper coins.   4 pieces
158 NOLA. Head of Minerva, olive and owl on helmet; rev. Minotaur standing to r., NΩΛΛ. Didrachm. Rare.
159 CAMPANIA (in general). Head of Hercules to r., on neck, lion's-skin and club; rev. she wolf suckling Romulus and Remus, in Ex. *ROMANO*. Splendid didrachm.

(There is little doubt about the origin of coins of this class. They were made in Illyria and other parts of Greece on purpose for Roman circulation, and sent to the Latin cities as an article of commerce. Many, like some that follow, were parts or multiples of the As.)

160 —— Helmeted head of Hercules to r., in the field club; rev. Victory holding a branch of palm and pointing to a prize, *ROMANO*. (Called *Victoriatus* by Pliny.) Splendid. Didrachm.
161 —— Janus bifrons in beaded circle; rev. Quadriga with Jupiter and Victory. (Called *Quadrigatus*.) Ex. fine and rare. Tridrachm.
162 —— Same type. Didrachm. Equally fine.
163 —— Helmeted head of Pallas to r., X.; rev. the Dioscuri galloping to r. Very fine. Denarius.

Greek Coins.

CAMPANIA. Helmed head to r., V.; rev. as before, in exergue *ROMA*. Fine and rare. Quinarius.

—— Head of Pallas; rev. owl; head of Mars; rev. cuirass; head of Mercury; rev. prow; head of Neptune; rev. Prow; head of Hercules; rev. prow; head of Mercury; rev. Caduceus. Copper coins, perfectly and beautifully patinated. 6 pieces

—— Helmed head of Mars; rev. trophy; Minerva; rev. owl, and others. Rare and fine. C. 4 pieces

—— Others. Equally fine, same class. 4 pieces

—— Head of Cybele with turreted crown; rev. Diana on horseback; head in lion-skin hood, to l. club; rev. dolphin, oscan legend. Fine and rare. C. 2 pieces

—— Head of Mercury with the pileus on his head; rev. prow. C. Beautifully patinated. Size 13

—— Head of Pallas to r.; rev. dog. Two varieties, and one with horse galloping. Very fine. C. 3 pieces.

CUMAE. Female head to r. bound with a fillet; rev. the monster scylla, *NΩIMΓX*. (Read backward.) Well preserved (not fine) and very rare. Didrachm.

CALES. Helmeted head of Pallas to l.; rev. cock crowing, Latin legend, *CALENO*, in field *. C. size 14

MAMERTIUM.

RHEGIUM. Double female head, *bifrons*; rev. helmed head of Pallas in hollow square; another; lion's head facing; rev. two olive leaves, *PH*. Beautiful. Hemidrachm. 2 pieces

—— Double head, diademed fronts, crowned with modius; rev. Jupiter seated, *PHITINΩN*. Very rare. Not fine.
C. size 16

NUCERIA. Helmeted and bearded head of Mars to l., to r. branch of olive; rev. upright bridled head and neck of a horse, at the base *ROMANO*, in the field, ear of barley. Of the highest rarity. Very fine. Didrachm.

—— Head of Pallas to l.; rev. horse head bridled, behind "Roman." C. Ex. fine.

LUCANIA.

177 POSIDONIA. Naked figure striking to r., *ΠΟϟΕΙΔ*; rev. bull, between his legs shell, *IEϟΟΠ* (from r. to l.), the letters *Δ* and *Σ* placed as they are found in the oldest inscriptions. Very fine example of an equally rare coin. Didrachm.

178 HERACLIA. Head of Pallas r.; rev. Hercules and lion struggling. Two varieties. Hemidrachm.   2 varieties

179 —— Head of Pallas l.; rev. infant Hercules strangling serpents; with another, obv. full face; rev. Hercules and Nemosan, lion struggling. Very rare. Hemidrachm.
2 pieces

180 THURIUM. Helmeted head of Pallas with Syren on Casque; rev. taurus Cornupetous to r., above *ΘΩΤΡΙΩΝ*, in ex. boar's head, *ΕΠΡΑ*. Of the most beautiful fabric, thick plated coin, the ancient fraud revealed only by the rusting of the copper within, with which exception in splendid condition. Extremely rare and valuable. Tetradrachm.

[The coins of Thurium in this collection are magnificent; fine specimens are marked at high figures, one in the Thomas sale many years ago having brought £21. The tetradrachm described cost 100 francs in 1828.]

181 —— Head Pallas to r., olive on helmet; rev. bull tossing to r., above *ΘΤΤΙΩΝ—Ε*; in Ex. fish. Didrachm.

182 —— The same. Syren on helmet; rev. in hollow. As it came from the die, billon. Didrachm.

183 —— The same. A wonderful work of art. The above type varied in the execution. Didrachm.

184 —— Head of Pallas to r., Syren on helmet; rev. bull tossing, *ΘΩΤΡΙΩΝ — ΝΥ* in field. Very fine. Didrachm.

[NOTE.—This cost 48 francs. It is not to be found in mionet.]

185 —— The same. Under *ΘΩΤΡΙΩΝ-ΣΙΜ*. Didrachm.

186 —— Head of Pallas to r., olive; rev. bull tossing to l., in hollow. Very fine. Hemidrachm.

187 —— Repetition of last. Only fine.

188 —— Head of Parthenopeia to l., behind bunch of grapes; rev. taurus to l. Sharp and perfectly patinated. A gem.
C. size 12

Greek Coins.

189 THURIUM. Repetition of last. Fine.
190 —— Head of Pallas to r.; rev. figure crowning trophy. C. 3 pieces
191 —— Head of Arethusa to l., wreath of sedge and wheat; rev. taurus tossing, above, a dolphin. And others of types already described. C. 3 pieces
192 —— Silver and copper, two of each. 4 pieces.
193 VELIA. Head of Pallas to r., griffon on helmet; rev. lion overpowering a stag with long branching antlers, VEAH-TΩN; planchet irregular, work and preservation magnificent. Very rare variety. Didrachm.
194 —— Head of Pallas to l., olive on helmet; rev. as last. Didrachm.
195 —— Head of Pallas to l., griffon; rev. lion eating ram's head, above, ΦI and grasshopper, VEAHTΩN, in exergue. Rare variety and very fine. Didrachm.
196 —— Obv. as last; rev. lion eating to l., above Λ., in exergue, VEAHTΩN. Didrachm.
197 —— Head of Pallas to r., griffon; rev. lion walking to r., ΦI, and 5-pointed star above; in exergue, VEAHTΩN. Very rare and fine. Didrachm.
198 —— Head of Pallas to l., on helmet, dolphin, Φ on neck and E in field; rev. lion walking to r., ΦI and trident above, VEAHTΩN in exergue. Fine and rare variety. Didrachm.
199 —— Head of Mercury, with pileus to r.; rev. lion passing to r. Small, thick coin, very fine. Gold.
200 —— Helmeted head to l.; rev. punch-mark in four compartments. Small, thick coin, very fine. Gold.
201 —— Female head, hair in net to r.; rev. owl on olive branch, VEAH. Fine and extremely rare. Drachm.
202 METAPONTUM. Head of Ceres to left, with braided hair; rev. ear of wheat, on blade, mouse, MET; all in hollow. Extremely beautiful. Didrachm.
203 —— Head of Ceres to r.; rev. ear of wheat, unknown symbols in field, META. Extremely fine head. Didrachm.
204 —— Head of Ceres; rev. wheat ear and crane to r., METAHON. Head very large and work very fine. Didrachm.
205 —— Head of Hercules in lion's skin to r.; usual reverse Copper patinated and extremely fine. Size 10

Greek Coins.

CALABRIA.

206 TARENTUM. Two men on horseback, naked and without arms, riding to l.; rev. Taras on dolphin's back carrying a round shield, holding in right hand a figure of Victory, below, waves; (see coin of Camarinas, engraved on p. 60, Humphreys' Coin Col. Manual); as it came from the die, and extremely rare. Didrachm.

207 —— Hercules naked riding l., club in left hand; rev. Taras astride of a dolphin holding diota and palm; in field, helmet, TAPAΜ (Sigma on face), above, ΘΙ. As rare as last and equally fine. Didrachm.

208 —— Nude horseman to r., holding wreath, to l. ΣΩ, below, NEY; rev. Taras on dolphin, behind, star, TAPA. Magnificent. Didrachm.

209 —— Horseman riding l., above, cap, below ΝΟΚΡΔ-ΗΣ; rev. Taras astride dolphin, in right hand trident, in left robe; something like a winged spur in field, waves below, TAPAΣ. As it came from the die. Didrachm.

210 —— Armed cavalier galloping to r., ΦΙ; rev. man with crowned head and sceptre riding dolphin to l., below, waves, in field eagle standing, ΘΙΑΙΣ. Perhaps the most interesting and valuable of the series. Large didrachm.
Size 14

211 —— Horseman, with palm, riding left, above EY, below YIITIAN; rev. Neptune carrying trident and Victory on dolphin to l., in field bunch of grapes. Extremely fine. Didrachm.

212 —— Obv. as last; rev. Neptune, with trident, striking l., behind owl, TAPAΣ. Didrachm.

213 —— Diademed female head, with earrings, to l.; rev. Taras on horseback, dolphin below, TA. Fine and rare. Didrachm.

214 —— Naked man, with Macedonian shield, sitting on horseback with both legs front; rev. Taras on dolphin carrying Minerva's helmet, TAPAΣ, water below. Another with Taras veiled, holding the acrostoleum and sceptre. Both rare. Didrachms. 2 pieces.

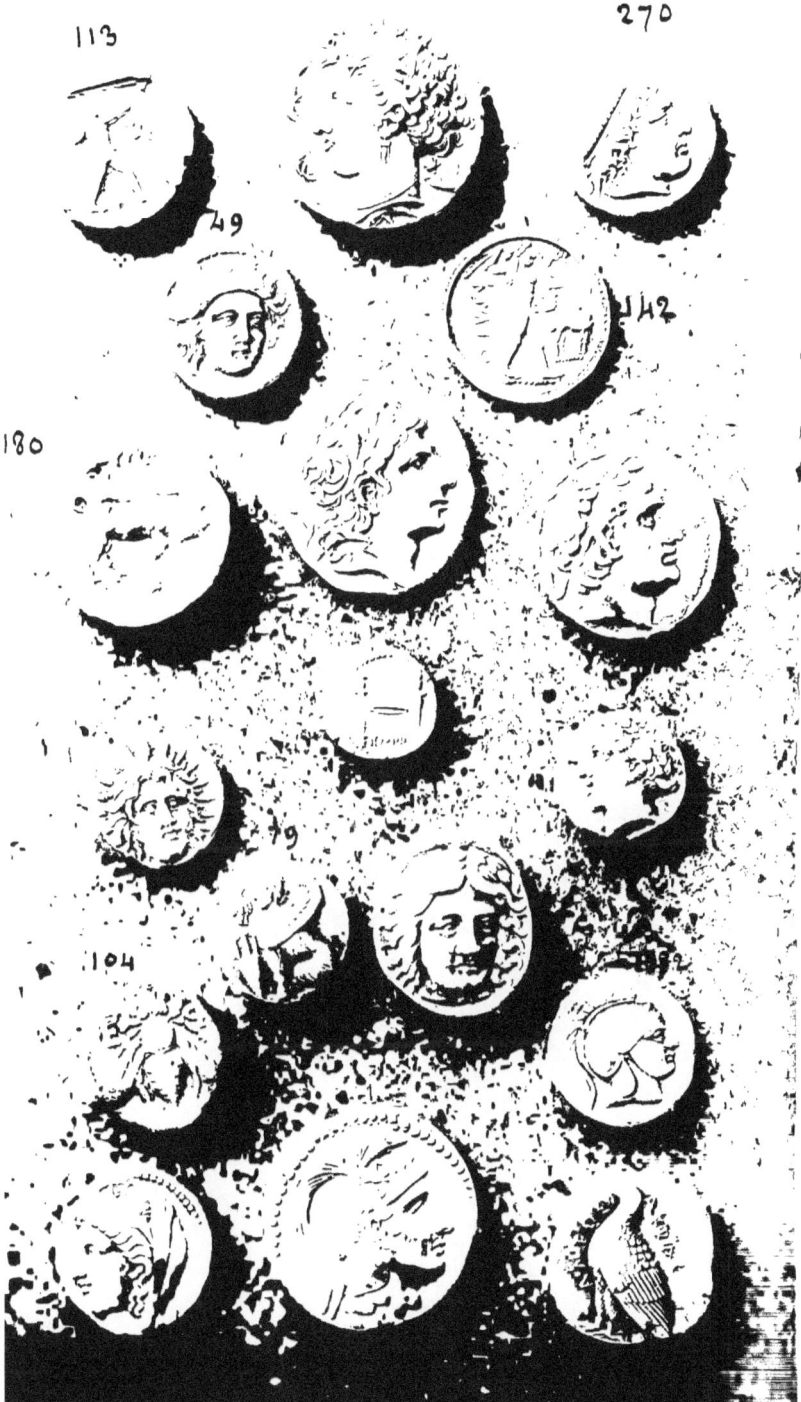

215 TARENTUM. Helmed head of Pallas (syren) l.; rev., owl on olive branch, wings *raised*. Another with wings *folded*. Very beautiful and rare. Drachms. 2 pieces

216 —— Head as before, r. and l.; rev. *TAPANTINI, large* owls, wings as before. Very fine and rare drachms. 2 pieces

217 —— Obv. diota and tripod; rev. diota; S., diobolus and obolus. 2 pieces

218 —— Tarus on dolphin; rev. bivalve. Very fine and rare. C. Size 8

219 BRUNDUSIUM. Laureated head of Neptune to r., behind trident; rev. Arion on dolphin with lyre and Victory, *BRVN*. Fine, well patinated and rare. C. Size 12

220 —— Obv. as before; rev. Arion on dolphin, lyre in hand, to l., monogram below, *BRVN*. C. Thick coin. Size 13

221 —— Head of Neptune, behind trident and Victory, below o o o o; rev. Arion on dolphin's back, Victory and lyre in hand to l., club, below *BRVN* and o o o o. Triens. C. Size 12

BRUTTIUM.

222 CAULONIA. Nude figure striking right, his left arm extended to r., stag to l., *KAVA* (reversed); rev. stag standing to r., olive to l., *AVAK*, read from right to left. Of great antiquity and in surprising preservation. Didrachm.

223 CROTONA. Pallas, full face; on helmet, syren, to r., *KPO*.; rev. Hercules, nude, reclining on lion's skin, in right hand diota, in field club and bow. Extremely rare. Didrachm.

224 VALENTIA. Head of Hercules to r.; rev. winged thunderbolt, in field two clubs, *VAAENTIA*. C. Size 16

225 TERINA. Female head to r., *TEPINAION*; rev. winged Victory seated, a bird with wings raised on his hand. Very rare. Didrachm.

226 —— Male head crowned with the Modius to r.; rev. standard, *TE*. Very small. C.

227 BRUTTIUM (*in general*). Diademed head of Juno veiled to r., to l., sceptre and bee; rev. Jupiter standing nude, resting

Greek Coins.

one foot on low altar and one hand on lance; to r., *BPET-TIΩN* to l., eagle; all in beaded circle. Nothing superior to it in the collection. Didrachm.

228 —— Arethusa, nearly full face, with a tiara of mushrooms, shells, and parsley, two dolphins on each side; rev. soldier charging to r., covered by shield; legend uncertain. A most remarkable coin, and one which will prove valuable. It has been taken for copper, because covered by red rust, but it is silver. Drachm. Well preserved.

229 —— Laureated head of Jupiter to r., to l. thunderbolt; rev. warrior with lance and shield to r., *BPETTIΩN*. Very fine. C. Size 15

230 —— Obv. as last; rev. eagle with raised wings. Very fine. C. Size 14

231 —— Helmeted head of Mars l.; rev. Pallas charging r. Very fine. C. Size 16

232 —— Another, same type, except o o o o. Very fine. C. Size 16

233 —— Head of Ceres to l.; rev. Jupiter hurling thunderbolt, in the field cornucopiae, *BIETTIΩN*. Very fine. C.

SICILY.

234 AGRIGENTUM. Eagle standing, legend reading from r. downwards, *AKPAC—ANTOΣ*, *Boistrophedon*; rev. in hollow, crab. Tetradrachm. Very rare.

235 —— Eagle standing, *AKRACANTOS*, reading properly; rev. in hollow, crab. Didrachm.

236 —— Eagle rending a hare; rev. crab and dragon. Drachm.

237 —— Eagle standing, *AK AR*. Hemi-drachm.

238 —— Eagle devouring hare; rev. crab and fish; and another, poor. C. 2 pieces

239 ENNA. Woman's head to r.; rev. bull standing to r., behind him a figure, below *H*. Pierced and poor, but rare. Drachm.

240 —— (Perhaps Camarina.) Swan and lizard, below *H*; all in dotted circle; rev. punch-mark. Very fine. Hemi-drachm.

Greek Coins. 23

241 SEGESTA. Greyhound standing r., ΣΕΓΕΣΤ; rev. woman's head, her hair coifed in four rolls; around ivy. Didrachm. Very rare.

242 SYRACUSE. Head of Hercules with lion-skin hood, ΣΥΡΑ; rev. deep incusum, in centre head of Arethusa, in corners ΕΥΡΑ. Splendid. Gold. Extremely rare. Size 7

243 —— Head of Arethusa or Proserpine with necklace, earrings and crown of sedge, dolphins around; above, ΣΓΡΑΚΩΣΙΩΝ, in field shell; rev. Quadriga, Victory crowning the driver; in exergue suit of armor. Didrachm, weight 767½ grs. Extremely fine and rare; cost 500 francs in gold. × Decadrachm

[There are on the reverse of this medal, under the base line, letters which undoubtedly compose the maker's name, but without a hint from some other source it would be difficult to determine what the name is. Of these beautiful medallions the whole number existing is not large, and certainly there are very few as fine as this.]

244 —— Head of Arethusa, four dolphins around; rev. quadriga, as before, triquetra above, in exergue ΣΥΡΑΚΟΣΙΩΝ. Very fine tetradrachm.

245 —— In hollow, head of Arethusa and dolphins; rev. quadriga of mules, Victory crowning the animals. One of their earliest coins. . Extremely fine tetradrachm.

246 —— Head of Arethusa (?) bound with pearls, hair in net, name reversed and upside-down; rev. charioteer in biga. Victory flying above. Extremely fine tet.

247 —— Head of Arethusa, four dolphins around, ΣΥΡΑΚΟΣ-ΙΟΝ; rev. biga and Victory to r., in exergue sea serpent. Very rare variety, and very fine tetradrachm.

248 —— Head of Minerva, long hair in net and fillet of pearls, ΣΑ-ΡΑΚΟΣΙΟΝ; rev. figure on horseback, in dotted circle; obv. in hollow. Extremely rare. Drachm.

249 —— Bearded filleted male head, in beaded circle r.; rev. beginning r. at bottom reading upwards to l. ΣΥΡΑΚΩΣΙΩΝ, woman holding hasta and sistrum; laurel'd head of Neptune l.; rev. winged figure in a biga; laurel'd head of Arethusa, to l. thunderbolt; rev. Pegasus. C. Fine. 3 pieces

250 —— Head of Pallas to l., ΣΥΡΑ; rev. two dolphin heads and tails together, between them a star of eight points. Thick coin of the clump form. C. Size 20

Greek Coins.

251 GELAS. Fore part of a human headed bull (the Minotaur), ΓΕΛΑΣ; rev. biga, Victory crowning the horses. Tetradrachm.

252 —— Minotaur, very long beard, the letters CEΛΛ, in primitive form, scattered at random between his legs; rev. horseman. A very early coin, in fine preservation. Didrachm.

253 —— Minotaur to r., above CEΛΛΣ; rev. helm'd horseman galloping to l.; another, obv. same; rev. bridled horse (lead) to r., to l. civic crown. Very fine and rare. Hemidrachm. 2 pieces

254 PANORMUS. Head of Ceres l., collar, necklace, and earrings; rev. horse standing r., full stater. Gold.

255 —— Repetition of last, except metal. Electrum.

256 —— Head of Ceres l. with wheat ears and earrings, in beaded circle; rev. horse to r., in beaded circle. Hemistater. Gold.

257 —— Obv. same; rev. horse looking back. Hemistater. Gold.

258 —— Palm-tree; rev. head and neck of horse, in beaded circle. Half size of last. Gold.

259 —— Head of Arethusa or Proserpine l., earrings and fillet of sedge, four dolphins around; rev. head and neck of horse l., to r. palm-tree, below Coptic letters. Very beautiful and rare. Tetradrachm.

260 —— Head of Ceres l., wheat ears and earrings; rev. horse standing r. Extremely fine and rare. Didrachm.

261 —— Head and neck of horse to r., in field torch; rev. head and neck of horse; another, head of horse to r., *bridled*, to l. ΠΑΝ. As they came from the die. Small. Silver. 2 pieces

262 —— Head of Ceres l.; rev. horse with breast-plate and collar, one fore-foot lifted, head with crescent and horn turned back; obv. same; rev. horse before a palm-tree; obv. same; rev. horse before a palm-tree; rev. horse and Ceres; rev. horse-head. From lot of rare coins. C. 5 pieces

263 —— Similar coins. Indifferent. C. 5 pieces

NOTE.—Some of these coins may belong to Carthage. It is useless to pretend to separate them.

Greek Coins. 25

264 TAUROMENIUM. Laureated head of Apollo to r., to l. bird; rev. tripod, *TAVPΩMENITAN.* Exquisite work on both sides. As it fell from the die. Gold. Size 6

265 —— Obv. same; rev. lyre. Copper. 2 pieces

266 ZANCLES (afterwards Messana, then Mamertini). Head of a man in hollow; rev. bivalve; dolphin, and tortoise in hollow; rev. bivalve; oblong, rounded corners. Small and extremely rare variety. Silver. 2 pieces. Size 5x7

267 —— Dolphin and Victory in hollow; rev. bivalve; dolphin; rev. bivalve. Silver. 2 pieces

268 MAMERTINI. Laureated head of Apollo to r.; rev. eagle standing, wings raised; in field star of seven points, —ΩN. Patinated and very fine. C. Size 14

269 —— Head of Apollo l.; rev. in hollow, eagle on thunderbolt, *MAMEΓ*—; obv. same; rev. warrior with long lance standing beside his horse, *MAMEΓTINIΩN*; bearded head of Jupiter to r.; rev. soldier with lance and shield to r., *MAM*, etc. Copper. 3 pieces

GREEK REGAL COINS.

MACEDONIA.

270 ARCHELAUS I., from 413 to 399 B C. Filleted head of Archelaus to r.; rev. bridled horse walking, r. APXAAO. Extremely fine and rare. Tetradrachm

271 AMYNTAS II., from 392 to 371 B.C. Head of Jupiter Ammon; rev. eagle in hollow square. Beautiful little coin. Gold.

272 PHILIP II., 359 to 366 B.C. Laureated, beardless head to r.; rev. biga to r., between horse's legs vase; in exergue ΦΙΛΙ-ΠΠΟΥ. Has been mounted as a gem, still fine. Stater, gold.

273 —— Laureated bearded head of Jupiter Ammon to r.; rev. the king on horseback, to l. wheel, in field, OO. Of extremely coarse fabric, yet in fine preservation. Very rare. Tetradrachm.

274 —— Laureated head of Jupiter r.; rev. the prince on horseback; to r. Φ, etc.; in exergue *N.* Ex. fine. Tetradrachm.

275 —— Same type. Drachm.

276 —— Same type. Copper. 2 pieces.

26   *Greek Coins.*

9.50   277   ALEXANDER III. (the Great), 336 to 324 B.C. Helmeted head
Hnz   of Pallas, earrings, to r.; rev. Victory, with trident stand-
              ing l. ΑΛΕΧΑΝΔ ΡΟΚ. Very fine stater ; gold.

4.25   278   —— Obv. same ; rev. thunderbolt, bow, and club, ΑΛΕΧ,
Finius   etc. Small gold (hemi-stater).

3.00   279   —— Head of Hercules, with the lion-skin ; rev. Jupiter
              Aetophorus seated ; to l. vase with one handle, and vine
Palmer   with two bunches of grapes ; in field, monogram, to r.
              ΑΛΕΧΑΝΔΡ. Pierced, but very broad and rare variety.
              Tetradrachm.   Size 21

3.00   280   —— Obv. same ; rev. Jupiter Aetophorus as before ; in field,
Strot   Bœotian shield. Very fine. Tetradrachm.   Size 15

3.25   281   —— Obv. same ; rev. Jupiter, etc., as before ; legend,
Hnz   ΒΑΣΙΛΕΩΝ ΑΛΕΧΔΡΟΥ, from bottom, round right
              hand to top. Extremely fine, and equally rare variety.
              Tetradrachm.

3.50   282   —— Obv. same ; rev. Jupiter as before, usual legend in
Snow   usual form. Very fine. Tetradrachm.

1.75   283   —— Obv. same ; rev. same, except in field pegasus. Ex-
Hnz   tremely fine and rare. Drachm.

1.00   284   —— Obv. same ; rev. same, except for pegasus monogram.
Strot   Equally fine. Drachm.

Hnz {.25   285   —— Obv. same; rev. same. Well preserved and rare.
              Hemidrachm.

"   *.25*   286   —— Obv. same ; reverses varied. All fine drachms.
                                                 3 pieces.

.10   287   —— Head of Jupiter Axur (radiated) ; rev. two cornu-
Leff —   copiæ, ΒΑΣΙΛΕΩΝ ΑΛΕΧ, etc. Struck in Egypt.
              Not fine, but very rare.   C., Size 14

15   288   —— Variety of copper (or rather fine brass) coins, such as
Chute   female head; rev. monogram. Male head ; rev. mule or
              zebra. Do. ; rev. bow, club, &—?. Macedonian shield
              with monogram ; rev. apex, bow and club. Small Size.
                                                 4 pieces.

lu   289   —— Head in lion-skin ; rev. bow, quiver, club, and torch
Mathews   (like those used in the Mystery of Ceres and Proserpine).
              A brass coin, apparently struck from dies for gold stater, as
              fine as possible, beautiful.

Greek Coins.

1.00   290   PHILIP ARIDAEUS (half brother of Alexander III.), from 324
Stub   to 317 B.C. In all respects like those of Alexander, except
             in the legend, which is ΦIΛIIIIIOΓ; and in exergue,
             BAΣIΛEΩN. An ancient forgery, hardly at all worn,
             and the base interior not perceptible, except in one minute
             spot. Tetradrachm.

3.25   291   —— Obv. same, the hood curiously elaborated ; rev. Jupiter
W Forrest   Aetophorus, tripod and monogram in circle. Fine and rare.
             Tetradrachm.

.50   292   —— Obv. same; rev. Jupiter seated; in field, torch.
Haz   Drachm.

.60   293   —— CASSANDER, from 316 to 298 B.C. Head of Hercules in
Mathews   lions skin ; rev. prince on horseback, above BAΣIΛEΩI,
             below KAΣΣANΔPY; in field two monograms. A very
             beautiful coin, large drachm size. C., or brass of fine
             quality.

.53   294   —— Same in all respects. Sage green patination. Size 12 *Anitton*
.10   295   —— Obv. same ; rev. lion couchant.   C., Size 11 *Deff*
1.00   296   PHILIP III., from 298 to 297 B.C. Laureated head to r. ;   *"*
             rev. man on horseback, below club, ΦIΛIIIIΩΓ. Small
             drachm S.

EGYPT.

1.75   297   PTOLEMY I. (Soter), B.C. 285. Diademed head of Jupiter; *Mathews*
             rev. eagle on thunderbolt, to l. cornucopiæ, BAΣIΛEOΣ
             ΠTOΛEMAIOY. Thick coin. Extremely fine.
                                                     C. Size 29

1.00   298   —— Same in all respects but in size.   Size 26 *Barush*
3.50   299   —— Diademed head of Ptolemy to r.; rev. eagle on a *Sorou*
             thunderbolt, to l. ΠTOΛEMAIOY; in field monogram and
             club. Tetradrachm.

3.25   300   —— Obv. same ; rev. eagle as before, ΣΩTHPΩΣ added *Frisier*
             to legend. Tetradrachm.

1.00   301   —— Obv. same ; rev. BAΣIΛEΩT added to legend, various *Palmer*
             monograms. Base. Tetradrachm.

2.5   302   PTOLEMY II. (Philadelphus), from 285 to 246 B.C. Young *"*
             head to r. ; eagle on thunderbolt—with others of the large
             Ptolemy family, long haired and short haired, with one or
             more eagles on the reverses. A fine lot.   C. 4 pieces.

.10   303   —— Other coins of this eminent family.   4 pieces. *Stick*

SYRIA.

304 SELEUCUS I. (Nicator), from 312 to 282 B.C. Diademed beardless head to r., within bearded circle ; rev. Apollo (?) seated on the cortina, sceptre and bow in hand, ΒΑΣΙΛΕΩΣ ΣΕΛΕΤΚΟΥ. Various monograms in field. Fine, broad, and very rare. Tetradrachm. Size 20

305 ANTIOCHUS I. or II., from 282 to 247 B.C. Laureated and bearded head of Jupiter to r. ; rev. eagle with cornucopiæ standing to l., with the name of Antiochus. Copper. Size 11

306 SELEUCUS III. (Ceraunus), from 227 to 224 B.C. Diademed beardless head to r. ; rev. Apollo seated (see Seleucus I.) Extremely fine. Tetradrachm.

307 ANTIOCHUS III. (the Great), from 223 to 187 B.C. Diademed beardless head to r. ; rev. Diana (?) seated on cortina, bow and arrow in hand, at her feet a hound. ΒΑΣΙΛΕΩΣ ΑΝΤΙΟΧΟΥ, with various monograms. Extremely fine. Tetradrachm.

308 SELEUCUS IV. (Philopater), from 187 to 176 B.C. Diadem'd head to r.; rev. Apollo seated. Of full size and weight, but defaced by rust. Rare. Tetradrachm.

309 ANTIOCHUS IV., from 176 to 164 B.C. Diadem'd head with long hair to r.; rev. eagle on thunderbolt, ΒΑΣΙΛΕΩΣ ΑΝΤΙΟΧΟΥ ΘΕΟΥ ΕΠΙΦΑΝΟΥΕ in four lines. Fine thick coin of the 1st size. C. Size 18

310 DEMETRIUS I. (Soter), from 163 to 161 B.C. Diadem'd beardless head to r. ; rev. half-draped female with cornucopiæ and wand; the throne on which she is seated rests on the figure of a winged syren, ΒΑΕΙΛΕΩΣ ΔΗΜΗΤΡΙΟΥ ΣΩΤΗΡΟΕ; monograms to l. and in ex. A piece broken off above the head ; otherwise in fine condition. Tetradrachm.

311 DEMETRIUS II. (Nicator), from 146 to 126 B.C. Diadem'd portrait to r.; rev. eagle standing to l., palm, club, and various monograms. Only fair. Tetradrachm.

312 —— Woman's filleted head ; rev. quiver and bow, on edge a ring of knobs. Rare and fine. C. Size 12

Greek Coins. 29

313 ANTIOCHUS VI. (Epiphanes), from 146 to 143 B.C. Radiated head of Apollo to r.; rev. double cornucopiae, stippled inscription in three lines. C. Size 1

314 TRIPHON (Autocrator), from 143 to 138. Portrait to r.; rev. symbols of royalty, *ΒΑΣΙΛΕΩΣ ΤΡΥΦΩΝΟΣ ΑΥΤΟ-ΚΡΑΤΟΡΟΣ*. Pierced, but of the very highest degree of rarity. (R 8). Drachm.

315 ANTIOCHUS VII. (Evergetes), from 138 to 127 B.C. Young head within beaded circle; rev. symbols of royalty, name in full as Evergetes. Rare and fine. C. Size 12

316 ANTIOCHUS IX. (Philopator), from 113 to 96 B.C. Portrait to r. in beaded circle; rev. Victory with palm to l., *ΒΑΣΙΛΕΣ ΑΝΤΙΟΧΥ*. C. Size 12

317 PHILIP (Philadelphus), about 95 B.C. Laureated beardless portrait to r.; rev. Jupiter Nicephorus (victorious) seated l., stippled inscription in four lines. Pierced, but fine. Tetradrachm.

THRACE.

318 LYSIMACHUS, from 324 to 292 B.C. Filleted head of Apollo to r.; rev. Pallas Nicephorus seated to l., *ΒΑΣΙΛΕΩΣ ΛΥΣΙΜΑΧΟΥ*, in exergue winged trident. Nearly as it came from the die. Very rare. Stater. Gold.

319 —— Diadem'd head with horns of Jupiter Ammon to r. (portrait); rev. same as last, except in field a caduceus. Nothing in ex. Very fine. Tetradrachm.

320 —— Young head to r. with fillet and horns of Jupiter Ammon, in beaded circle; rev. Pallas Nicephorus seated, her shield with the gorgon face supporting her left arm, in the field a spear, *ΒΑΣΙΛΕΩΣ ΛΥΣΙΜΑΧΟΥ*. Extremely fine. Much more rare than last. Drachm.

NOTE.—Without doubt this coin bears the head of Agathocles, son of Lysimachus. It is one of the gems of the collection.

PARTHIA.

321 ARSACES. Uncertain date. Clothed bust with bearded filleted head in beaded circle; rev. in hollow, king seated to r. holding bow, behind, dagger, *ΒΑΣΙΛΕΩΣ ΒΑΣΙΛΕΩΝ ΜΕΓΑΛΟΥ ΑΡΣΑΚΟΥ ΕΠΙΦΑΝΟΥΣ*. Letters stippled. Broad drachm. Size 12

322 ARSACES V. (Phraates I.) Crowned bust in jeweled robes, long pointed beard ; rev. ΒΑΣΙΛΕΩΣ ΜΕΓΑΛΟΥ ΑΡΣΑΚΟΥ ΦΙΛΟΠΑΤΟΡΟΣ ΕΠΙΦΑΝΟΥΣ ΦΙΛΕ-ΛΛΗΝΙΟΣ. The sitting figure and accessories as before. Broad drachm. Size 12

323 ARSACES VI. (Mithridates I.), from 155 to 140 B.C. Obv. similar to last; rev. similar to last, except for *Philopater, Evergetes.* Drachm. Same size.

PERSIA.

324 ARTAXERXES, from 226 to 240 A.D. Crowned head to r., legend in Persian characters; rev. on high altar, bust; priest on each side. Drachm. Fair condition. Size 14

325 SAPOR I., from 240 to 271 A.D. Bust of Sapor crowned ; rev. altar and priests ; on obv. two circles ; on rev. three do. Drachm. Very fine. Size 18

326 —— Barbarous head to r. ; rev. Gothic *A* and two globules. Thick coin. Gold. Size 11

PONTUS.

327 MITHRIDATES VI. (Eupator Dionysius), from 123 to 62 B.C. Diademed head of Mithridates to r.; rev. Pegasus grazing ; to l. crescent and star ; to r. ΕΣΩΝ. ΒΑΣΙΛΕΩΣ ΜΙΘΡΑΔΑΤΟΥ ΕΥΠΑΤΟΡΟΣ, all within wreath of ivy and vine leaves. Nearly as it came from the die. Extremely beautiful and rare. Tetradrachm. Size 20

> NOTE.—Mithridates was one of the greatest *collectors* of ancient times. He was called *Eupator* because he had a good father, and *Dionysius* in compliment to Bacchus, and for the same reason may have adopted the *ivy* wreath, which is always found on his coins.

CARIA.

328 MAUSSOLUS (died about 353 B.C.) Laureated head of Apollo, full face ; rev. a figure of Jupiter Labradaeus, wearing the pallium, holding in his right hand the bipenne, and his left the hasta pura, ΜΑΥΣΣΩΛΛΟ. As fine and rare as anything in the catalogue. Tetradrachm.

BITHYNIA.

329 PRUSIAS, 187 to 149 B.C. Young head wearing the pileus ; rev. Caduceus, ΒΑΣΙΛΕΩΣ ΠΡΟΥΣΙΑΣ. C. Size 9

SICILY.

DIONYSIUS, *Syracuse?* uncertain date. Fore part of a horse running, l. Victory on the wing holding a wreath over his head; to r. trinacria; to l. sprig, *ΔΙΟΝΤΣΙΩ*; rev. palm tree, six Phœnician letters; all in circle of dots. Extremely fine and rare. Tetradrachm.

NOTE.—Humphrey says "no coin can with certainty be attributed to Dionysius, or Dionysius II." Yet this is a genuine coin, and sufficiently Sicilian in character to make the attribution legitimate.

AGATHOCLES, from 317 to 289 B.C. Head of Proserpine, necklace, earrings, knot and tassel; to r. *ΣΩΤΕΙΡΑ*; rev. *ΒΑΣΙΛΕΟΣ ΑΓΑΘΟΚΛΕΟΣ*. Very fine. C. Size 15

—— Same in all respects, except dark green patination.

HIERO II. 269 to 215 B.C. Head of Ceres l., r. torch; rev. biga, *ΙΕΡΩΝΟΕ*; between horses' legs *Π*. A perfect gem. Gold. Size 10

—— Diademed head of Hiero l.; rev. cavalier with lance, galloping r., name and monogram in exergue and field; and one with bearded head; rev. trident. C.- 2 pieces

—— Duplicate of one in last lot (the first), twice struck, so as to form double profile. Extremely fine. C. Size 17

PHILISTIS, uncertain date (probably wife of Gelo, son of Hiero II.) Diademed head veiled; rev. biga to r., the horse trotting, Victory in the chariot, *ΒΑΣΙΛΙΣΣΑΕ ΦΙΛΙΣΤΙΔΟΣ*. Nearly as fine as when struck. Much rarer than tet. Drachm.

(Cost 40 francs.)

PHINTIAS, *Agrigentum*, 280 B.C. Head of Proserpine to l.; rev. wild boar at bay, *ΒΑΣΙΛΕ-ΦΙΝΤΙΑ*; and one laureated male head, rev. two eagles devouring a hare. Very fine and interesting coins. 2 pieces. Size 13

CYRENAICA (*Africa*).

PTOLEMAEUS (Apron), died 96 B.C. Bearded head of Jupiter Ammon to r.; rev. the sacred sylphium plant. Fine and *extremely* rare. Thick coin. C. Size 16

MAURETANIA.

JUBA I., contemporary with Julius Cæsar. Bearded head to l.; rev. horse running. Copper. Size 17

32 *Greek Coins.*

340 JUBA II., from 30 to 19 B.C. Diademed head of Juba to r. paludamentum and sceptre, *REX-IVBA*; rev. temple. plated coin (ancient forgery). Denarius.

CAPPADOCIA.

341 ARIOBARZANUS AND ARTABAZARNUS (Philoromæus). Diademed beardless head to r.; rev. Pallus Nicephorus (bearing Victory) to l., legend inclosing the figures in lines at right angles. Drachm size. S. Fine and rare. 2 pieces.

THE ROMAN COINAGE.

THE "AS" OR ÆS" AND ITS DIVISIONS.

COPPER.

342 AS LIBRALIS. Head of Janus, bifrons; rev. prow of a ship, 1. Deeply patinated. Size 43

343 SEMIS. Laureated, bearded head, below S.; rev. prow, S. Deeply patinated. Size 36

344 TRIENS. Helmeted head, four globules; rev. prow, four globules. Well patinated. Size 32

345 QUADRANS. Laureated head in hood, three globules; rev. prow, three globules. Well patinated. Size 28

346 SEXTANS. Head, with pileus, two globules; rev. prow, two globules. Well patinated. Size 24

347 UNCIA. Helmeted head, one globule; rev. prow, one globule. Well patinated. Size 18

348 FULL SERIES. Reduced size, bearing heads of Janus, Pallas, Mars, Hercules, and Mercury; all with ROMA globules, and the other proper characters to indicate the denomination. *Very fine,* and in this form rare. Perfectly and beautifully patinated. 6 pieces.

349 As. Cross in high relief; rev. the same. Size 18

350 —— Laureated head; rev. prow. Rare. " 24

351 TRIENS. Dolphin, ●●●●; rev. thunderbolt, ●●●●. Rare. Size 32

352 QUADRANS. Boar running, ●●●; rev boar running, ●●●. Rare. Size 28

353 UNCIA. Head of Apollo, full face, Nimbus and rays, ●.
rev. crescent and two stars, with 8 points, ●. ROMA.
Finely patinated, and rare.   Size 16

MULTIPLES OF THE "AS."
SILVER.

354 QUADRIGATUS. . A Triple Denarius, Head of Janus; rev.
Quadriga, ROMA (letters incuse). Fine and rare.
Size 16
(See Humphrey's Manual, p. 272.)

355 DOUBLE DENARIUS. Same type, different work. Extremely
fine, very rare.   Size 14

356 DENARIUS. Head of Pallas, winged helmet, behind X.; rev.
the Dioscuri, with long lances galloping to r., in Ex. Roma.
Fine.   Size 12

357 DENARII. Varieties belonging to Rome, not attributable to
particular families, striking and remarkable types, no
duplicates.   10 pieces

358 QUINARIUS. Head of Pallas, V to l.; rev. the Dioscuri Roma.
Fine and rare.   Size 11

359 SESTERTIUS. Head of Pallus, 11.S. (2½ as) to l.; rev. like last,
as it came from the die. *Very* rare.   Size 8

360 VICTORIATUS. Head of Mars; rev. Victory Crowning a
trophy; and *female* head, same reverse; the latter a Quinarius.
Both fine and rare.   2 pieces.

361 SERIES of the foregoing: Double Denarius, Denarius, Quinarius, and Sestertius. A rare lot.   4 pieces.

COINS OF ROMAN FAMILIES.

NOTE.—As many of the denarii in the following series have the
fine and inimitable polish that time gives to perfect coins, whose
surfaces have been protected from injurious contacts, the term
brilliant will be used to distinguish such from those even *extremely* fine. It has never before been my good fortune to cata
logue, or even to see, so fine a collection.

362 ABURIA. Head of Rome, GEM; rev. Victory in Quadriga,
M ABVRI, ROMA. Very fine.

363 ——— The same; rev. Armed Charioteer, same legend. Very
fine.

Coins of Roman Families.

364 ACCOLEIA. Draped female bust, filleted head, P ACCOLEIVS, LARISCOLVS; rev. the Sisters of Phæton changing into larch trees. Very fine.

365 ACILIA. Female head with laurel crown, hair in knot, necklace, and earrings, SALVTIS; rev. Hygiea standing, serpent in hand, one elbow resting on cippus, IIIVIR VALEV AV ACILIVS. As it came from the die.

366 —— Another, same as last. Brilliant.

367 AELIA. Head of Rome, X; Diana in chariot drawn by two stags, in field crescent, in Ex. ROMA. Very fine.

368 —— Same; rev. Dioscuri on horses, P. PAETVS—ROMA. Very fine.

369 AEMILIA. Camel standing, man on one knee extending palm branch, M. SCAVR AED CVR; rev. P. HYPSAERES AED-CVR driving to l. in Quadriga, in Ex. CHYPSAE COS PRIV-RES ARETAS. Very fine.

370 —— Veiled head of Vesta, PAVLLVS-LEPIDVS-CONCORDIA; rev. Lepidus standing beside a trophy, behind it Perseus, King of Macedon, and his two sons, prisoners. PAVLLVS-TER. Brilliant.

371 —— Head of Juno, laureated and diademed r,, ROMX; rev. Equestrian statue on the bridge "Sublicius," built by Ancus Martius, LEP in the arches, long, oval. Ex. fine.

372 —— Another of this type. Equally fine.

373 AFIANIA. Head of Rome, X; rev. biga, S AFRAN–ROMA; as it came from the die in sharpness; patination of a fine brown color, very rare, on silver.

374 ANNIA. Two hands crossed over a caduceus, SILIVS-ANNIVS-LAMIA; rev. SC AAA FF II VIR. Copper (denarius size). Beautifully patinated.

375 ANTESTIA. Head of Rome; rev. Dioscuri riding, dog running before the horses, ROMA. Very fine.

376 —— Same; behind, CRAG. to r. X; rev. Jupiter in Quadriga, l. ANT, below ROMA. Very fine.

377 ANTIA. Bust of Hercules, laureated and bearded, behind club; rev. horseman riding two horses over a bridge, below a mouse, letters incuse on bridge; TI—(C Antius Restio). Fine. Rare.

Coins of Roman Families. 35

378 ANTONIA. Head of Mars, laureated and bearded, SC, in beaded circle ; rev. Quadriga, with Victory holding olive branch and palm, RQ ANT BAR. Coin with serrated edge. Ex. fine.

NOTE—Silver coins were sometimes dentilated in the mint, to make the circulation of plated coins (counterfeits) more difficult. Tacitus speaks of the preference given to these coins by the Germans.

379 —— Head of Juno veiled ; Caduceus held by two hands clasped, M ANT C CAESAR. *Quinarius.* Also another same size, obv. cock and vase (præfericulum); rev. Victory crowning trophy. Both misstruck, yet in good preservation, and very rare. 2 pieces.

380 —— Head of Anthony, M-ANT-IMP–AVG-III VIR-R-RO-M. BARBAT-QR; rev. head of Octavian, CAESAR-IMP-PONT–III.VIR-R-P-C, all in beaded circle, fine and sharp, but pierced. Very rare.

381 —— Galley, with 12 oars shown, ANT-AVG III-VIR, R.P.C.; rev. Eagle between two standards, counter stamped with *camel* over the number of the legion, but assumed to be the 1st, another instance of the patination already noticed. Very fine. Rare.

382 —— Galley, 15 oars, LEG. II.   Extremely fine.
383 ——   "   12 "   LEG. III. Equally fine.
384 ——   "   10 "   LEG. IV.   "   "
385 ——   "   " "   LEG. V.   Very good
386 ——   "   " "   LEG. VI. Extremely fine.   "
387 ——   "   14 oars, LEG. VII. Equally fine.   "
388 ——   "   15 "   LEG. XI. Brilliant.   "
389 ——   "   " "   LEG. XX. Fine.

A magnificent and rare series not easily formed.

390 APRONIA. APRONIVS-SISSENNA A.A. A.F.F. SC.; rev MESSALA BAL, etc.—(Moneyer of Aug), anvil. Copper. Very fine, and very rare.

391 AQUILEIA. Head of Apollo, radiated, X.; rev. Diana in biga, above Crescent and 4 stars, star under horses. MAN AQVIL ROMA. Very fine.

392 —— Helmeted head of Mars, beardless, VIR.III. VIRTVS; rev. a soldier victorious, his vanquished enemy on the ground supporting himself by one hand. SICIL M. AQVIL. Brilliant.

Coins of Roman Families.

393 ATILIA. Head of Rome, X.; rev. biga, Victory, whip in hand, driving; SAR. ROMA. Ex. fine.

394 —— Head of Rome, SARN. X,; rev. Dioscuri, M-ATILI ROMA. Very fine.

395 AURELIA. Head of Rome, ROMA. X. to r. M-AVRELI; rev. biga, soldier launching a javelin, SCAVRI—LICIN DOM. Serrated edge. Extra fine.

396 —— Head of Rome, COTA; rev. biga drawn by Centaurs. M AVRELI, ROMA. Good specimen. Very rare.

397 BABIA. Head of Rome, TAMPIL; rev. Quadriga, Apollo with bow, BÆBIAQF. ROMA. Ex. fine.

398 BETILIENA. S.C. P. BETILIENVS BVSSVS; rev. Altar, III. Vir. etc. (a moneyer of Augustus), small C. Very fine, and beautifully patinated.

399 CAECILEA. Crowned and bearded head of Bacchus (?), Q. METEL—PIVS; rev. Elephant walking to r., SCIPIO IMP. Very fine. Rare.

400 —— Head of Rome, Q, MET; rev. Jupiter in Quadriga, the horses stepping, Roma. Very fine.

401 —— Head of Rome; rev. small shield, with elephant's head; round the shield, P.F. M METELLIVS. Very fine. Rare.

402 —— Head of Rome, ROMA; rev. two elephants harnessed, C. METELVS. Very fine, and rare type.

403 CALIDIA. Head of Rome in beaded circle; rev. biga, Victory driving at full speed. M. CALID, Q. ME.C.N.L. Very fine.

404 —— Variety of same type. Very fine.

405 CALPURNIA. Laureated head of Apollo, N. in beaded circle; rev. horsemen riding at full speed, in field Caduceus, L.PISO FRVGI. Brilliant.

406 —— Variety, same type. Very fine.

407 —— Same head, to r. vase; rev. Victory walking to l. L.PI, below, FRV. As it came from the die. Quinarius.

408 CARISIA. Head of Moneta, MONETA; rev. in olive wreath, implements for coining money—anvil, hammer, and pincers, T CARISIVS. Brilliant. Very rare.

409 —— Head of Rome, ROMA in beaded circle; rev. within wreath, anchor, cornucopia, and other objects unknown. Brilliant.

Coins of Roman Families. 37

410 CARISIA. Head of Venus; rev. Sphinx T CARIS III VIR. Very fine.

411 CARRILIA. Head of Rome; rev. Quadriga, driver carrying a lighted torch, CARR. ROMA. Very fine.

412 CASSIA. Female head, long hair, to l. Sceptre; rev. eagle on thunderbolt, to r. præfericulum, to l. simpulum, Q. CASSIVS. Extremely fine.

413 —— Veiled head of Vesta, Q. CASSIVS; rev. circular temple of Vesta, A.C. on tablet to r., to left, vase; Pierced and somewhat abused, but little worn. Rare.

[This is said to refer to L. Cassius Longinus (whose name appears on next coin), who brought two vestal virgins to judgment, and condemned them. This explains the significance of the temple and head of Vesta on coins of this family.]

414 —— Veiled head of Vesta and lamp; rev. Longinus Sacrificing, LONGINVS. Very fine. Rare.

515 —— Head of Liber, crowned with vine; rev. head of Ceres crowned with ivy, behind, thyrsus; beaded circle on both sides. Very fine.

[Bacchus was worshiped with Ceres, and accounted her inseparable companion—So virgil joins them together, *Liber and Alma-Ceres*, for it is by them we have wine and corn—Mystagogus Poeticus.]

416 —— Head of Rome; to l. præficulum; rev. Quadriga at full speed, C. Casse Roma. Very rare.

417 CIPIA. Head of Rome, X. M.CIPI-MF.; rev. biga, ROMA. Very fine.

418 —— Duplicate of above.

419 —— Plated coin of this family, same type. Very fine. Rare.

420 CLAUDIA. Head of Ceres, lyre; rev. Diana holding two hastæ, a lighted torch on end of each, P. CLODIVS MF. Ordinary.

421 —— Beautiful head of Diana, quiver and bow, SC.; rev. biga, charioteer holding wreath and palm, horses flying, A. C XXII, in Ex. CLAVD T.I.F. Dentilated edge. Extremely fine.

422 —— Head of Rome, chariot, with three horses prancing. A.P.C.LT. Brilliant.

423 —— Duplicate of last, and one PVLCHER in exergue Extremely fine. 2 pieces.

424 —— Falsification, and small patinated copper. Very fine. 2 pieces.

Coins of Roman Families.

425 COELIA. Head of Rome l., in beaded circle; rev. biga L. C. COIL. in Ex. CALD, above C. in beaded circle. Brilliant.
426 —— Duplicate. Extremely fine.
427 —— Same; rev. biga to r., woman driving, victory crowning her; on one of the horses, star of 8 points; P. CALD. Very fine.
428 CONSIDIA. Female head to r.; rev. *Sella Curulis* (Chair of State), above, C. CONS. in Ex. PAETI. Extremely fine. Rare.
429 COPONIA. Head of Venus, Q'SICINVIS III VIR; rev. lion skin and club between arrow and bow, C. COPONIVS. Good. Very rare.
430 CORDIA. Owl standing on helmet, RVFVS; rev. shield bearing head of Medusa, CORDIVS. Extremely fine, rare.
431 —— Heads of the Dioscuri, RVFVS. IIIVIR; rev. Justice blindfold, holding hasta and balance, a small winged figure on her shoulder, M. CORDIVS. Brilliant.
432 —— Duplicates of last. Very fine.   . 2 pieces
433 CORNELIA. Head of Sulla. SVLLA COS; rev. head of Pomponius Rufus, with his name as Consul. As it came from the die.
434 —— Head of Diana. FAVSTVS; rev. Sulla on a throne, two figures kneeling, one a prisoner, the other presenting a branch of olive, FELIX (in allusion to the surrender of Jugurtha, by Bocchus, king of Mauretania). Extremely rare. A fine coin.
435 —— Head of Juno, with laurels, diadem and sceptre, S. C. rev. Sulla's signet, "Three Trophies." (placed on coins struck under the influence of Faustus, Sulla's son.) Extremely fine and rare.
436 —— Sella Curulis (double chair), with lituus and crown, SVLLA COS; rev. Sella Curulis, arrow and laurel, Q. POMPEIVS. QARVFVS—COS. Extremely fine, rare.
437 —— Head of Victory, MANLI P. RII Q.; rev. Sulla in a triumphal car, the horses going slow, Victory crowning the conqueror, SVLLA IMP. Beautiful.
438 —— Helmeted, beardless head, to l. crown, to r. BLASIO—CNF; rev. warrior in arms, receiving honors from attendants. Another, with head and club of Hercules; rev. trophy. Another, with laureated head bearded; rev. Jupiter in Quadriga, SCIP. ASIA. G. Coins with allusions to victories over Mithridates in the East. All fine. 3 pieces

Coins of Roman Families. 39

439 CORNELIA. Head of Rome; rev. biga with winged Victory, the horses frightened, C W LENTVLVS. Nearly as it came from the die.

440 —— Quinarius. Ancient forgery. Another, genuine. Both of Lentulus. Extremely fine. 2 pieces

441 —— Head laureated and bearded, behind sceptre (?); rev. globe, anchor, thyrsus and crown, C N LEN Q. Splendid.

442 COSSUTIA. Head with fillet and wings, S. ABVLA; rev. Bellerophon on Pegasus hurling a lance, xvi. COSSVTI. S F.

443 CREPUSIA. Laureated head, cluster of grapes and thyrsus; rev. Cavalier galloping to r., in exergue P. CREPVSI. Very fine.

444 —— Duplicate. Misstruck, but fine.

445 CUPIENNIA. Head of Rome to l., cornucopia to r.; rev. Dioscuri, V. CVP. ROMA. Brilliant.

446 —— Others. Strictly fine. 2 pieces

447 CURIATIA. Head of Rome X Q. CVR. T; rev. Jupiter in Quadriga, M SIA—ROMA. Extremely fine.

448 —— Head of Rome, TRIO; rev. C. CVR. F ROMA. Fine.

449 CLOULIA. Head to r.; rev. Victory crowning trophy, T CLOVLI Q. Quinarius. Extremely fine.

450 —— Head of Rome, to l. crown; rev. biga. the horses rearing, to r. car of wheat, T CLOVLI. Very fine. Denarius.

451 DIDIA. Head of Rome, RA; rev. two soldiers fighting, T DIDI. Very fine.

452 DOMITIA. Head of Rome, X. ear of barley, in beaded circle; rev. biga, under the horses man contending with lion, C. N. DOM. above, ROMA. Very fine.

453 —— Head of Rome, X. to r., ROMA; rev. Quadriga, the horses walking, C N DOM. Long oval. Very fine, rare.

454 EGNATIA. Diadem'd head of Apollo, MAXSVMVS. in field a malleus; rev. between two prows, two soldiers with long lances, C. M. M. CE. EGNATIVS CNF. long oval coin. Fine and rare.

455 EGNATULEIA. Laureated head, C. EGNATVEL CF; rev. Victory hanging shield on trophy; below litnus, ROMA. Quinarius. Fine and rare.

456 FABIA. Laureated head of Apollo, in field Lyre; to l., ROMA Q MAX.; rev. in laurel wreath, cornucopia and thunderbolt crossed. Extremely fine.

40   *Coins of Roman Families.*

457 FABIA. Veiled head of Cybele, X within beaded circle; [rev. Victory in biga, under the horse a crane, C. FABI. C. F. A remarkable and very fine coin.

458 —— Head of Rome to r., X LABEO; to l., ROMA; rev. Jupiter in Quadriga, in Ex. Q FABI. Very fine.

459 —— Head of Rome, X; rev. bearded figure seated, half draped, with helmet, spear and shield; on the last, QVIRINI, in right hand Apex, Q. FABI, to l., PICTOR, in Ex. ROMA. Rare and very fine.

460 FANNIA. Head of Rome, ROMA. X.; rev. Victory in Quadriga at full speed, M.F.N.C.F. As it came from the die.

461 —— Duplicate. Extremely fine, and another.   2 pieces

462 FARSULEIA. Head of Juno, necklace and diadem, MENSOR, in beaded circle; rev. Mars in biga, handing in a priest, FARSVLEI. Brilliant.

463 FLAMINIA. Head of Rome, ROMA X.; rev. Victory in biga, L.FLAMINI, in Ex. CILO. Ex. fine.

464 —— Duplicate. Fine.

465 FLAVIA. Head of Rome; rev. biga FLAVI; in Ex. ROMA. Very fine.

466 FONTEIA. Young head laureated, hair in curls, M. FONTEI C.F. below, thunderbolt, all in beaded circle; rev. within olive wreath, cupid riding a goat; in field, caps and stars of Dioscuri, in Ex. thyrsus. Large and very fine.

467 —— Janus bifrons, to l. C., to r. star; rev. large galley, the commander conspicuous above the rowers, 5 oars, C. FONT ROMA. As from the die.

468 —— Heads of Dioscuri; rev. galley, 12 oars out, M FONT. Extremely fine, rare variety.

469 —— Young head laureated, thunderbolt below, M FONTEI C.F.; rev. in large olive wreath, Cupid on a goat, cap and star on each side, in Ex. thyrsus. Extremely fine.

470 —— Helmeted head of young warrior, trophy behind; P. FONTEIVS PA CAPITO III VIR. in beaded circle; rev. mounted warrior riding down an enemy, small nude figure beside the vanquished; in beaded circle. Brilliant.

471 —— Examples of foregoing varieties. Very fine.   3 pieces

NOTE.—Coins of the Fonteia family are held as valuable. See Mionet.

Coins of Roman Families. 41

472 **Fufia.** Heads accolated, one laureated, one helmeted. FALENI. HO.VIRT; rev. male and female figures face to face, the former (Italy personified) holding a sprig, the latter (Rome), one foot on ball—to l., Caduceus. Serrated edge; countermarked and slightly bent, but fine. Rare.

473 **Furia.** Head of Ceres, wreathed with wheat ears, stalk of the same to l., to r. kernel, III VIR. BROCCHI. in beaded circle; rev. fasci to r. and l. of the sella curulis (double consular seat), I. FVRI. C. N. F. Brilliant and beautiful.

474 —— Janus bifrons, L. F. M. FVRI.; rev. Victory crowning trophy, PHILI ROMA. Very fine.

475 —— Head of Rome; rev. Diana in biga, FVR-ROMA, in field a ? Fine.

476 **Gellia.** Head of Rome in broad laurel wreath; rev. man and priest in quadriga, C.N.GFL ROMA. Very good.

477 **Herennia.** Female head diademed, PIETAS; rev. naked figure bearing draped figure on his shoulders, M HERENNI. Very fine, also rare.

NOTE.—See story of Æneas; also the "Pii Fratres," Anapias and Amphinomus.

478 **Hosidia.** Head of Venus, GETA. III VIR.; rev. wild boar wounded, dog worrying him, C.HOSIDI. C.F. Notched edge, very fine.

479 **Hostilia.** Head of Pallor; rev. Diana holding stag by his horns, SASERNA-L. HOSTIL. Ordinary.

480 —— Head of Venus, crowned with roses; rev. Mercury or Victory, with Caduceus and trophy, SASERNA - HOSTILIVS. Extra fine.

481 **Julia.** Elephant in Ex. CAESAR, in beaded circle; rev. implements of sacrifice. About as it came from the die, rare.

482 —— Head of Rome, CÆSAR; rev. two winged Victorie harnessed to Cæsar's triumphal car, in field, crescent. Same condition as last, very rare.

483 —— Diademed head of Venus; rev. double cornucopia and Victory, VALENTIN. Splendid preservation.

NOTE.—Cæsar had been in Aegypt, whose queens had for generations used the double cornucopia as their symbol.

484 —— Head of Venus as before; rev. Æneas carrying his father, Anchises, from burning Troy; in right hand, the palladium, CÆSAR. Discolored by red oxide, but sharp and beautiful. Very rare.

485 JULIA. Winged female head, trident; rev. Victory in Quadriga in Ex. L JVL BVRSI. Extremely fine.

486 —— Head of Rome, anchor; rev. Julius triumphing, Victory crowning him, above ROMA, below SEX JV. Fine.

487 JUNIA. Young female head, PIETAS; rev. two hands clasping a caduceus ALBINVS. BRVTI. F. Brilliant. Rare.

488 —— Head of Rome; rev. Victory in biga D. SILANVS ROMA. Brilliant.

489 —— Female Head. LIBERTAS; rev. four figures marching to l.; understood to be Junius Brutus between two lictors, preceded by a herald; in Ex. BRVTVS. Extremely fine, very rare.

490 —— Head of Rome; rev. Dioscuri, C JVNI, and another of same type, M JVNI. Very fine. 2 pieces

491 LICINIA. Diademed and laureated head of Juno, car-rings and necklace S. C.; rev. man standing by a horse. P CRASSVS. M.F. Beautiful, rare.

This coin is supposed to relate to the inspection of the horses of the Equites by the Censors.

492 —— Jupiter hurling a triple thunderbolt; rev. Pallas in Quadriga, spear and shield. C. LICINIVS LF. MACER. Brilliant.

493 —— Head of Rome. C.O.S. COM. FX.; rev. warrior in biga, lance and shield. C. LICINI. M. F. Brilliant.

494 LIVINEIA. Head of Regulus, REGVLVS, in beaded circle; rev. Sella Curulis, and 6 fascii L. LIVENEIVS REGVLVS. Beautiful.

495 LUCILLIE. Head of Rome, to l. PV, in laurel wreath; rev. Victory in a biga whipping the horses. M. LVCILI. Brilliant.

496 —— Duplicate (no other type of this family). Very fine.

497 LUCRETIA. Radiated head of Apollo (or Diana); rev. crescent and seven stars. LVCRETI. TRIO. Brilliant.

498 —— Head of Rome. TRIO; rev. Dioscuri C. N. LVCR. ROMA. Brilliant.

499 —— Others. C. T. E. R. LVCR. and CN.LVCR. Beautiful. 2 pieces

500 LUTATIA. Head of Rome, Greek helmet. CERCO. ROMA; rev. Galley. Q LVTATI. QA. within wreath of oak leaves and acorns. Brilliant.

Coins of Roman Families. 43

501 MAENIA. Head of Rome, X.; rev. Victory in Quadriga, P. MAE-ROMA, and one with different cognomen. Very fine. 2 pieces
502 —— Duplicate. Very fine.
503 MAIANA. Head of Rome; rev. Victory in biga, driving the horses with a whip. C. MAIANI. ROMA. Very fine.
504 MAMILIA. Head of Mercury, to L. Caduceus; rev. Ulysses, recognized by his dog, MAMIL LIMETAN. Brilliant.
505 —— Another, slight variety. Extra fine.
506 MANLIA. Helmeted head to L. MANLI. PRO Q; rev. Quadriga, Victory crowning driver. L SVLLA. Very fine.
507 —— Duplicate. Finer, but broken on edge.
508 MARCIA. Head of Ancus Marcius, in bandalet. ANCVS. Litnus above; rev. equestrian statue on a bridge. AQVAM between the arches. Above, PHILIPPVS. Very fine, rare.
509 —— Head in a horned cap (pileus), rev. equestrian statue, as before. PHILIPPVS on the base. Very fine.

NOTE.—The above coins of the Marcia family commemorate the building of the aqueduct which carried the stream of water called the Aqua Marcia, to Rome.

510 —— Head of Honor in laurel crown; rev. nude figure of Silenus, with skin bottle of wine; to r. column, C CENSOR. Brilliant.
511 —— Accolated heads of Numa Pompilius and Ancus Marcius; rev. postillion and led horse. XVIII. CENSOR. Very fine, rare.
512 —— Head of Rome; rev. armed horseman galloping. Q. PHILIPP. Brilliant.
513 —— Head of Rome; rev. biga, wheat ears upright under horses. MARC. ROMA. Another, Dioscuri riding. Behind head, LIBO. Very fine. 2 pieces
514 MARIA. Head of Ceres. CAPIT. CXXXVIII; rev. two oxen in plough. Above, CXXXVIII. Below, C. MARI. C. S.C. In good preservation, rare.
515 MEMMIA. Head of Ceres. C. MEMMI. C. F., in beaded circle; rev. in similar circle, kneeling captive supporting trophy. C. MEMMIVS. IMPEPATOR. Brilliant.
516 —— Laureated head of Apollo; rev. the Dioscuri standing beside their horses, preparing to start in opposite directions. MEMMI. Large and extremely fine denarius.
[See note to a coin of the Servillia family (No. 584).]

517 MEMMIA. Laureated head of Mars. S. ROMA; rev. figure in biga crowned by Victory. L. MEMI. CAL. Very fine.

518 MINUCIA. Beardless head, Greek helmet; rev. two soldiers fighting, a third down. Q. THERM. MI. Extremely fine.

519 —— Head of Rome, RVF ; rev. dioscuri. Q. MINV. ROMA. Very fine.

520 —— Same ; rev. Jupiter in Quadriga ; in Ex. MINV. Very fine.

521 —— Same ; rev. rostral column. Priests performing religious rites. MINVCCI. ROMA ; and another, rev. biga. Fine. 2 pieces

522 MUSSIDIA. Head of Apollo radiated ; rev. two priests on the deck of a galley; religious implements and ceremonies. Poor.

523 NAEVIA. Head of Rome ; rev. Victory in biga, C. NAIVAI. Very fine.

524 —— Head of. Venus; rev. Victory in triga C. NAE. BALB. Pierced.

525 NERIA. Head of Mars, NERI-QVRB ; rev. eagle between two standards. Fine, rare.

526 NONIA. Head of Pluto, S. C. SVFFENAS ; rev. nude figure seated on spoils, Victory crowning him. SEX. NON. Brilliant.

527 —— Another, same type, very different execution. Beautiful.

528 NORBANA. Head of Venus, C NORBANVS CXXXXVII ; rev. wheat head, fasces and caduceus. Extremely fine.

529 —— Same, except No., which is XXIII ; this is about as it came from the die.

530 OPEIMIA. Head of Rome, crown behind ; rev. Victory in Quadriga, holding large wreath, L OPEIM. Extra fine.

531 PAPIA. Female head in goat skin coif—plough ? rev. Griffon running to l, PAPI. Extra fine, rare.

532 PAPIRIA. Head of Rome, behind, sprig ; rev. Jupiter in Quadriga. M CARBO. ROMA. Very fine.

533 —— Same, Ex. behind X ; rev. Jupiter hurling thunderbolt from car. CARB. Splendid.

534 PETRONIA. Head of Feronia, goddess of the woods. FERON.—TVRPILIANVS—III VIR ; rev. Parthian captive kneeling, skin of wild beast over his shoulders ; standard in hand, CAESAR AVGVSTVS SIGN RECE. Extremely fine and rare.

Coins of Roman Families. 45

535 PINARIA. Head of Rome; rev. biga. NATA—ROMA. Very fine.
536 PLAETORIA. Head of Cybele, in Greek helmet. CESTIANVS SC; rev. eagle on thunderbolt. M PLAETORIVS MF AED CVR. Extra fine.
537 —— Head of Cybele in *turreted* helmet; rev. Consular seat. Same legend as before. Fine, rare.
538 —— Head with flowing hair; rev. Caduceus. Fine.
539 PLANCIA. Head with the Pileus, C.N. PLANCIVS AED CVR. SC; rev. Thyrsus and bow; to R., stag. Very fine.
540 PLAUTIA. Mask of Medusa, full face, to l., PLANCVS; rev Aurora conducting the horses of the sun, to l., PLANCVS. Brilliant.
541 —— Duplicate. Same in all respects. Equally fine.
   [Struck by L. Plautius Plancus, to commemorate a nocturnal enterprise of his ancestor, the Censor Plautius. See Humphrey, p. 280.]
542 —— Head of Cybele, turreted crown. A PLAVTIVS AED CVR-SC; rev. Bacchius kneeling beside a camel, holding up olive branch. BACCHIVS JVDAEVS. Brilliant.
543 —— Same. Extremely fine.
544 —— Head of Neptune. P. YPSAE-S.C.; rev. Quadriga. YPSAE COS PRIV CEPIT. As it came from the die.
545 —— Head of Rome; rev. Dioscurii riding. C PLVTI. Ex. fine.
546 —— Repetition of last, and one with Bacchius, etc. Fine. 2 pieces
547 POBLICIA. Head with Greek helmet; rev. warrior standing before a trophy. CMA. As it was coined. Rare.
548 —— Same type differently executed. Very fine.
549 —— Laureated head of Apollo; to l. METEL A. ALB. SF. Under bust, tortoise; rev. Rome sitting on spoils, Victory crowning her. M-A.ROMA. Extra fine.
550 —— Head with horned pileus; rev. Hercules straugling lion, at his feet, club. Q POBLICI. Very good, rare.
551 POMPEIA. Head of Rome; to l. vase; rev. a she-wolf suckling Romulus and Remus under a fig-tree; above, birds, the old shepherd, Faustulus, looking on with admiration. SEX POM (FOSTLVS), in ex. ROMA. Very fine and rare.

46 Coins of Roman Families.

Pomponia. Laureated head of Apollo; L., POMPON. MOLO. Rev., priest officiating at a sacrifice, attendant leading goat to the altar. NVM. POMPIL. Extremely fine, rare.

553 —— Another, equally fine.

554 —— Head of Rome. L POMPONI. C. NF. X. Rev., warrior with shield and ? in biga. L LICIN DOM. Brilliant.

555 —— Another, equally fine.

556 Porcia. Head of Rome. P LAECA X; rev., two men; lictor behind them. PROVOCO. Ordinary.

557 —— Head of Rome. LÆCA ; rev., victory crowning figure in biga. M PORC. ROMA. Brilliant.

558 —— Same ; rev., biga, C. CATO. Very fine, rare.

559 —— Head of Juno. M CATO ; rev., Victory seated, VICTRIX. Broken on one edge, otherwise as coined.

560 —— Same ; Quinarius. Very fine, rare.

561 Postumia. Head of Spain (personified), long hair and veil, HISPAN ; rev., priest consecrating eagle ; to r., fasces, in Ex., POST AF NS ABW. Has the lustre given by the dies, except in spots where the copper has corroded the the plate. It has a notched edge, which proves that the artifices of the ancient forgers were equal to the necessities of the case. A rare and beautiful ancient falsification.

562 —— Bust of Diana ; on draped shoulders, bow and quiver, in beaded circle ; rev., hound running, C. PVSTVM. A. Brilliant.

563 —— Head of Rome ; to l., Apex ; rev., Quadriga. L., POST. A ROMA. Very fine.

564 Procilia. Head of Juno Sospita, or Opipena, in goat-skin coif, S. C. ; rev., same goddess in biga, armed with shield and lance ; in field, L. PROCILI. F. Fine.

565 —— Head of Jupiter, laureated and bearded ; rev., Juno Sospita striking with lance, guarded by double shield ; at her feet, serpent. Very fine, rare.

Note:—L. Procilius, triumvir, was of Lanuvium, where *Juno Lanuvium* had a statue like the reverse of the last coin.—*See* Morell.

566 Quinctia. Bust of Hercules, club on shoulder, head laureated and bearded ; rev., Postillion with led horse ; below, rat, B. T. I— in ex., incuse letters, ? Very fine, but an ancient falsification.

Coins of Roman Families. 47

567 QUINCTIA. Head of Rome, behind, Apex; rev., Dioscuri, TQ.
    Very fine.
568 RENIA. Head of Rome, X. Rev., biga drawn by goats, C.
    REN. ROMA. Very fine.
569 ROSCIA. Head of Juno Sospita, goat-skin coif, ROSCI; to L.,
    vase; rev., girl feeding a serpent coiled before her, head
    raised, FABATI. Brilliant.
    [This girl represented the priestess at Lanuvium, in Juno's temple.
    See last note.]
570 —— Another; mint mark on obv., Scorpion; on rev., Crab.
    Brilliant.
571 RUBELLA. Beautiful little copper of a moneyer of this gens.
    Rare.
572 RUBRIA. Laureated head of Jupiter, DOSSEN; rev., Tri-
    umphal chariot, four horses going slow. L RVBRI. Bril-
    liant.
573 —— Head of Juno, diadem and veil, necklace, earrings and
    sceptre, DOS; rev., same as last. About as fine as pos-
    sible.
574 —— Head of Neptune; to l, trident, DOSSEN; rev., Vic-
    tory supporting large palm before an altar encircled by a
    serpent, his head raised above it, L., RVBRI. Extremely
    fine. Quinarius.
575 RUTILIA. Head of Rome, FLAC; rev., biga, L., RVTIL.
    Very fine.
576 SATRIENA. Head with Greek helmet, xxxv; rev., she wolf
    walking; above ROMA; in ex., SATRIENVS. Extremely
    fine, rare.
577 SAUFEIA. Head of Rome; rev., biga and Victory; L., SAVF,
    in ex., ROMA. Very fine.   2 pieces.
578 SCRIBONIA. Diademed head of Fortune, BON EVENT LIBO;
    rev., altar adorned with two lyres and a garland of flowers;
    above, PVTEAL; below, SCRIBON. Very fine.
    [To commemorate an altar erected by Scribonius Libo where a
    thunderbolt fell.]
579 —— Duplicate, with another, rev., Dioscuri. Fine.
                                                2 pieces.
580 SEMPRONIA. Head of Rome, PITIO; rev., Dioscuri, L.,
    SEMP. ROMA. Very fine.
581 SENTIA. Head of Rome, to l.; rev., Jupiter in Quad., thun-
    derbolt in hand, L., SATVRN, in beaded circle; as it came
    from the die.

582 SERGIA. Head of Rome, necklace and earrings, to l. ROMA ; rev., warrior riding at full speed, in his left hand a weapon and human head, M., SERGI ; in Ex., ROMA. Exactly as it was struck. *Rare.*

583 —— Duplicate of this type, but both sides different from last. Very fine.

584 SERVILIA. Head of Pallas, helmet, necklace and earrings, behind crown, in Ex., ROMA ; rev., Castor and Pollux riding in opposite directions. C., SERVEILI MF. Very fine.

> The Dioscurii are the same as the constellation "Gemini"—composed of two stars alternately above and below the horizon, one concealing itself when the other appears. It is explained that they are sometimes represented riding in opposite directions, to indicate the sojourn which they alternately make in the celestial and plutonian regions.

585 —— Bearded head bare, AHALA ; rev., bearded head bare, BRVTVS. Very fine and rare.

586 —— Beardless head, Greek helmet, RVLLI ; rev., biga, Victory with palm, horses prancing. P. SERVILI MF. Brilliant.

587 —— Head of Pallas, to l. litnus ; rev., mounted warrior fighting with one on foot. C., SERVEILI. Very fine.

588 —— Head of Rome ; rev., warriors fighting before their horses, the latter rearing; M SERVEILL Stain on obverse which can be removed ; rev., brilliant.

589 SICINIA. Head of Fortune, diadem, earrings, FORT. PR. ; rev., Caduceus and palm crossed ; above, crown. S- SICINIVS. Fine.

590 —— Head of Venus, diadem and earrings, below *. Q SICINIVS III VIR ; rev., lion skin, club and bow, C. CAPONVIS P. P. S. C. [See Caponia family.] As it came from the die. Rare.

591 SILIA. Bust of Diana, horned helmet, spear, and on her shoulder a magnificent buckler, crescent above, star in the field, to R., ROMA ; rev., in an inclosure, 3 figures partially draped. P. NERVA. Very fine.

592 SPURILIA. Head of Rome ; rev., biga, A SPVRI ROMA. Very fine.

593 STATILIA. Head of Pallas ; rev., biga. PVLCHER. Very fine.

594 SULPICIA. Veiled head of Vesta, SC. ; rev., implements used in sacrifices ; P. GALB. AE CVR, patinated with red oxide, but a fine denarius.

Coins of Roman Families. 49

595 THORIA. Head of Juno Sospita in goat's skin coif, SMR ; rev., bull bounding, THORIVS—BALBVS; above C. Very fine.

596 —— Marked variety of the same type. Very fine.

597 TITIA. Bearded winged head of Bacchus ; rev., Pegasus. TITI. Misstruck on obv., but extremely fine.

598 —— Duplicate. Very fine.

599 —— Head of Bacchante; rev., as before. Poor, rare.

600 —— Female bust, winged; rev., Pegasus on the ground, Q TITI underneath. Very fine Quinarius.

601 TITURIA. Bearded head, bare; to r., T (Monogram of Tatius, King of the Sabines,) behind, SABIN ; rev., two soldiers carrying off two women; in Ex. L., TITVRI. Very fine.

602 —— Head of Tatius as before, but without monogram, SABIN ; rev., woman on heap of shields, two soldiers holding shields above her; L., TITVRI. Extremely fine.

These coins illustrate the story of the rape of the Sabine women and the subsequent revenge of the Sabines on Tarpeia, daughter of the Roman governor, etc.

603 —— Same head ; rev., Victory in biga, L., TITVRI, in Ex., Cuirass. Very fine, rare.

604 —— Laureated head of Tatius, to l. O ; rev., Victory crowning trophy, P. SABIN. Extremely fine and rare Quinarius.

605 TREBONIA. Head of Rome, X ; rev., Jupiter in Quad., L. TRE–RA. Fine.

606 TULLIA. Head of Rome, ROMA; rev., Victory in Quad., M. TVLLI. Very fine.

607 VALERIA. Bust of Victory winged; bare head, necklace and earrings ; rev., Mars with lance and trophy standing between Apex and ear of wheat, L., VALERI FLACCI. Very fine.

608 —— Duplicate. Equally fine.

609 —— Head of Rome ; rev., biga ; above, FLAC, below, C VAL–C.

610 —— Winged bust of Victory, hair in net ; rev., Roman Eagle between two standards, CVAL FLAC EX. S.C. IMPERATOR. Fine, and extremely rare variety.

Coins of Roman Families.

611 VARGUNTEIA. Head of Rome, M VARG: rev. Jupiter with thunderbolt and palm in quadriga, the horses walking. Extremely fine.   2 pieces

612 VETURIA. Head of Rome, X. TI VET; rev. man on his knees, holding a sow between two soldiers, who touch the animal in token of an agreement, or treaty. ROMA in field. A very good coin, and rare.

613 VIBIA. Head of Pan, to l., *Pedum* (pastoral staff). PANSA; rev. Jupiter Anxur seated on a chair without back, holding in one hand a sceptre, and in the other a patera. JOVIS AXVR C VIBIVS. C. F. C.N. Extra fine.

614 —— Laureated head of Apollo, PANSA; rev. Minerva in full panoply, standing in Quadriga; the horses galloping; VIBIVS. C.F. Large oval coin. Brilliant.

615 —— Duplicate of last. Extremely fine.

616 —— Head of Bacchus crowned with ivy, PANSA; rev. Ceres carrying torches; (suggestive of her search after Proserpine in the Mysteries). C VIBIVS. CF. CN. Very fine, rare.

617 VOLTEIA. Laureated head of Jupiter; rev. Tetrastyle temple. M. VOLTEI. M.F. Extremely fine.

618 —— Head of a Bacchante, crowned with ivy; rev. Ceres, holding torches aloft, in biga, drawn by serpents (compare with coin of Vibia). M VOLTEI-M.F. Very fine and rare.

619 —— Head of Juno Sospita; rev. wild boar at bay. M. VOLTEI. Piece broken off, yet fine and desirable.

620 —— Female bust, the head with helmet crowned with laurels, behind cock; rev. Cybele in biga drawn by lions. M. VOLTEI.-M.F. Ancient falsification. Fine, rare.

ROMAN IMPERIAL COINS.
GOLD.

621 AUGUSTUS. Head of. CIVIBVS SERVATIS CAESAR COS VII; rev. eagle holding a wreath of oak between two branches of laurel. AVGVSTVS. S. C. Very fine.

[The Senate decreed that laurel trees should be planted before his house, and a crown of oak hung between.]

622 TIBERIUS. Head of. TI CAESAR DIVI AVG-F AVGVSTI; rev. seated figure holding hasta and olive branch. PONTIF-MAXIM. Extremely fine, rare.

Roman Imperial Coins.

623 HADRIAN. Head of. HADRIANVS-AVG-COS IIIPP; rev. Hope standing, holding flower. SPES AVG. Brilliant.

624 HADRIAN. Head of; rev. Jupiter Nicephorus (holding Victory), with hasta. JOVI VICTORI. Brilliant.

625 ALEXANDER. (Severus.) Head of. IMP-C-M-AVR-SEV-ALEXAND. AVG; rev. Mars armed, passing to r., P-M-TR-P.VII-COS-II-P.P. Brilliant.

626 TETRICUS. Head of. IMP TETRICVS. P. F. AVG; rev. Hope holding baton and flower. P.M. T-R-P. COS-P-P. Ex. fine.

627 THEODOSIUS. Bust of. DN THEODOSIVS P.F. AVG; rev. the emperor seated, holding sceptre and shield; inscribed on, VOT V MVL X. Legend CONCORDIA AVG. GGG. in Ex. CONOB. Brilliant.

628 ARCADIUS. Bust of. DN-ARCADIVS P.FAVG; rev. Emperor with labarum and Victory, one foot on fallen foe. VICTORIA AVGGGG., in Ex. CONOB. Very fine.

629 HONORIUS. Bust of. DN HONORIVS -P.F. AVG; rev. like last. Brilliant.

630 HONORIUS. Bust facing in helmet and mail; rev. Rome Nicephorus seated, star in the field. CONCORDIA. AVGGG., in Ex. CONOB. Brilliant.

631 VALENTINIAN. (Placidianus). Bust of. DN VPLAVALEN, etc.; rev. emperor holding cross and Victory, one foot on a severed head. VICTORIA AVGGG-RV., in Ex. CONOB. Ex. fine.

632 —— Obv. head; rev. Victory passing. Poor, Electrum.

633 ANASTASIUS. Bust, full face, holding sceptre. DN ANASTA-SIVS S-P.F. AVG; rev. Victory holding cross-staff, passing to L., in field, star. VICTORIA AVGGGA., in Ex. CONOB. Brilliant.

634 JUSTINIANUS. Bust, full face, with sceptre. DN IVSTINI-ANVS P.F.AVG; rev. like last, except in field, monogram of Christ. Brilliant.

635 —— Diademed bust to R.; rev. Victory with wreath and cross; in field, star. Beautiful, half aureus.

636 PHOCAS. Diademed bust to R., DN FOCAS PERAVG; rev. similar to last. Very fine, half aureus.

52   *Roman Imperial Coins.*

637 LEO III. Crowned bust, full face; in hand, globe surmounted with cross. LEON P AVG ; rev. crowned bust, full face, between stars. DN. CONSTANTIN. Very fine, half aureus.

638 CONSTANTIUS IV. Bust of Christ, front face, head Nimbused ; rev. two kings half length, both holding one double cross. CONSTANTIN. Extremely fine, full aureus.

639 CONSTANTINE. Bust, front face, with globe and cross. CONSTANTIN-SPP AVG; rev. double cross with crosslets on 4 steps. VICTORIA AVG. Pierced, but very fine aurens.

640 CONCAVE AUREUS ; obv. (convex side), Christ seated on throne ; rev. emperor standing crowned, and in his robes ; mund and labarum in his hands. Legend bilingual. Very fine coin. Size 19

ROMAN IMPERIAL.

SILVER.

641 POMPEY (the great). B. C., 49. Head of Pompey, between litnus and pefericulum. MAC PIVS IMP- ITER ; rev. Neptune, one foot on prow, standing between Anapias and Amphinomus, who are carrying their aged parents from the flames of Etna. Not squarely struck, consequently a part of the type, as described, wanting. Stained in spots by red oxide, but not at all the worse for wear. Very rare.

642 JULIUS CAESAR. B. C., 47. Head of Julius, laureated. CAESAR: M : MP.; rev. Venus standing, holding Victory and hasta. L BVCA. A very good example of this rare Denarius.

643 —— Helmeted head of Minerva. CAESAR ; rev. cupids on the wing, drawing a triumphal car ; in field harp; in exergue. I. IVLIVS L-F. Extremely fine, rare.

644 —— Head of Julius; rev. winged Victory over Cistus and serpents. ASIA RECEPTA, Quinarius.

645 BRUTUS (Marcus). B. C., 47. Head of Brutus. BRVT. IMP. L. PLAET CEST ; rev. cap between two daggers. EID MART. Extremely fine, rare.

646 ANTONY (Marcus). B. C., 47. Head of Marc Antony, M· ANTON IMP. AVG III VIR R.P.C. : rev. head of Octavius. C. CAESAR IMP. PONT. III.VIR R P.C. Preservation excellent, very rare.

[Yet this valuable coin is an ancient counterfeit, the inside being copper.]

Roman Imperial Coins.

647 ANTONY. Head of Antony, in field litnus; M ANTONINVS IMP COS, DESIG ITER ET TERT, all in wreath of ivy; rev. bust of Cleopatra on the Bacchic chest, between serpents entwined. RPC III VIR. Fine and extremely rare. Medallion. Size 16 — 4.00 *Cash*

[This coin was struck in Asia, where the worship of Bacchus prevailed, which explains the introduction of the *ivy* wreath, as well as the type of the Cistophorus. A coin is described where, in place of the bust of the Queen of Egypt, that of Bacchus is placed on the chest.]

648 —— Head of Antony, M ANTONINI VIR.; rev. temple of Apollo; within, radiated head of the god. III VIR R.P.C. Fine, rare. — 10/- *Assendix*

649 CLEOPATRA. Head of the Queen of Egypt; CLEOPATRAE REGINAE FILIORVM REGVM; rev. head of Antony; ANTONI ARMENIA DEVICTA. Very fair and quite desirable in a first-class cabinet. Very rare. — 50/- *Sternst*

650 AUGUSTUS. B.C., 31. Head of Augustus; rev. two laurel trees; above, CAESAR, below, AVGVSTVS. Fine, very rare. — 1.00 *Mathews*

[See note to gold coin of Augustus.]

651 —— Head; rev. a flaming star of 8 points or rays. DIVI JVLIVS. Fine. — 5/- *Anthony*

[Augustus obtained a decree of the Senate that Julius should be reckoned among the gods. This star was the token or sign of his deification. Augustus, very soon after, adopted the Capricorn as the symbol of his own rank among the stars.]

652 —— Head; rev. Apollo in a long tunic, lyre in hand. Very fine. Rare. — 1.00 *Inv.*

(Struck to commemorate the battle of Actium, before which he consulted the oracle of Apollo.)

653 —— Head, right and left, DIVI AVGVSTVS; rev. bull tossing, right and left, IMP X & IMP XII. Very good. 2 pieces — 5/- *Bal...*

654 —— Head; rev. the Prince riding, full speed; to left, eagle and standards; and another, with his grandsons, Caius and Lucius, shields and implements of sacrifice. Fine. 2 pieces — 40 *Have*

655 —— Head, IMP CAESAR DIVI.F. III VIR. ITER.; rev. Templ., DIVO. I - COS II - ITER ET TERT - DESIG, figure standing within, and altar near. Good, rare. — 60 —

656 —— Head; rev. implements of sacrifice. Fair, rare. — 20 *Preusky*

657 —— Head; rev. Victory erecting trophy. Fine and rare. Quinarii. — 20 *do*

54 Roman Imperial Coins.

658 TIBERIUS, A.D. 14. Head of Tiberius, TI CAESAR DIVI AVV F AVGVSTVS; rev. PONTIF MAXIM, woman (Julia or Livia) seated. Very fine.

659 —— Duplicate. Equally fine.

660 —— Duplicate. Same in all respects.

661 DRUSUS (Nero Claudius), brother of Tiberius. Head, NERO CLAVD DIVI CLAVD F CAESAR AVG, Victory standing and Victory seated on globe, ARMENIA. Fine, very rare. Quinarii. 2 pieces

662 GERMANICUS (son of Drusus). Head, GERMANICVS. P CAESAR AVG GERM; rev. Head of Caius (Caligula), C. CAESAR AVG GERMANICVS. Very fine, equally rare.

663 CALIGULA, A.D. 37. Head, CAIVS CAESAR GERMANICVS; rev. implements of sacrifice. Very good. Rare.

664 CLAUDIUS, A.D. 41. Head, TI.CLAVDIVS CAESAR AVGVSTVS. GERM; rev. S. P. Q. R. P.P. OB. CS. in wreath of oak leaves with acorns. Extremely fine, very rare.

665 —— Head; rev. Messalina standing, holding two children, Greek Imperial Medallion, in Potin, ΜΕΣΣΑΔΙΝΑ. Well preserved and very rare. Size 17

666 MESSALINA. Head of Messalina; rev. head of Claudius. Greek imperial medallion. Potin. Rare.

667 AGRIPPINA, JR., wife of Claudius. Head, AGRIPINAE AVGVSTAE; rev. head of Claudius, TI-CLAVD. CAESAR AVG. GERM P.M. TR. IE. PPP., beaded circle on obv. and rev. Extremely fine, very rare.

668 NERO, A.D. 54. Head, NERO CAESAR AVGVSTVS; rev. temple of Vesta, goddess seated, VESTA. Fine and very rare.

669 —— Head, rev. Health seated, SALVS. Ordinary, rare.

670 —— Head; rev. Jupiter seated, holding thunderbolt and hasta, JVPITER CVSTOS. Well preserved, rare.

671 —— Head crowned; rev. head of Tiberius, and one with head of Poppea, ΠΟΠΠΑΙΑΕ. Greek imperial. Potin. Both fine, rare. 2 pieces

672 GALBA, A.D. 68. Head, GALBA AVG; rev. S.P.Q.R. OB. C.S. within wreath. Well preserved, very rare.

673 —— Head, IMP SERG. GALBA CAESAR AVG; rev. figure, with hasta and patera standing; DIVIA AVGVSTA. Fine, rare.

Roman Imperial Coins.

674 OTHO, A.D. 69. Head, IMP OTHO CAESAR AVG; rev. Security standing, holding hasta and wreath. Very good and rare.
675 —— Head; rev. Ex. Mars standing, SC. Good, rare.
676 VITELLIUS, A.D. 69. Head, A VITELLIVS IMP. GERMANI-CVS; rev. tripod; above dolphin, below bird, XV VIR SACR FAC. Very good, rare.
677 —— Duplicate. Same in all respects, equally good.
(This tripod was only used by the Quindicemvirs, and related to the worship of Apollo, whose principal temple was at Dolphi, so named from the Dolphin:)
678 —— Obv. two hands crossed, FIDES PRAETORIANORVM; rev. same. Extremely fine and rare.
679 —— Head; rev. Victory carrying a globe, flying to left, VICTORIA AVGVSTI. Fine, rare.
680 VESPASIAN, A.D., 69. Head, CAESAR VESPASIANVS AVG; rev. vase with sheaf of wheat ears, IMP XIX. Extremely fine, rare.
681 —— Head; rev. the Emperor, as High Pontiff, seated on curule chair. PON MAX TRP COS VI. Very fine.
682 —— Duplicate, except the Emperor is seated on chair with high back; also one with rev. of Equity standing with scales. Both very fine, 2 pieces.
683 —— Head; rev. "Annona Augusta," and one rev. Pontifical Instruments, TRIPOT AVGVR. Ex. fine. 2 pieces.
684 —— Head; rev. Winged Caduceus, and one with the heads of Titus and Domitian facing. Very good and rare. 2 pieces.
685 —— Head; rev. double Capricorn under globe, and one with basket of grapes. Very good. 2 pieces.
686 —— Head; rev. Victory seated on globe. Very fine. Quinarius.
687 TITUS, A.D., 79. Head, T CAESAR IMP VESPASIANVS AVG; rev. Titus in a Triumphal Car, 4 horses walking, TRP VIII. COS. VII. Very fine. Rare.
688 —— Head; rev. Jupiter standing nude, holding hasta and patera, JOVIS CVSTVS. Very fine. Rare.
689 —— Quinarius; rev. Victory. Extremely fine. Rare. 2 pieces.

56   *Roman Imperial Coins.*

690 JULIA (daughter of Titus). Head of Julia, JVLIA AVGVS-
TA TITI AVGVSTI F; rev. Venus standing, leaning on
cippus, holding casque, VENVS AVGVSTA. Extremely
fine and rare.

691 DOMITIAN, A.D., 81. Head, IMP CAES DOMIT AVG
GERM. PMT. R; rev. Pallas marching. IMPXXII COS
XVII. As it came from the die.

692 —— Same; Pallas standing, IMP XVI. Equally fine.

693 —— Same; Pallas on prow. Equally fine.

694 —— Same; rev. Ceres standing with flowers. Extremely fine.

695 —— Same; rev. Burning altar garlanded, PRINCEPS
JVVENTVTIS. Equally fine.

696 —— Same; rev. On broad Cippus, LVD SAEC FEC COS
XIII, within laurel wreath. Very fine.

697 —— Same; rev. Delphine Altar, and one rev. Pegasus. Fine
and rare.   2 pieces.

698 —— Same; rev. various. Beautiful.   3 pieces.

699 DOMITIA (wife of Domitian). Head. DOMITIA AVGVSTA
IMP DOMIT; rev. Peacock, CONCORDIA AVGVST.
Very fine and rare.

700 NERVA, A.D., 96. Head; rev. Implements of sacrifices, viz:
litnus, præfericulum, flagellum, and simpulum. COS. III
PATER PATRIAE. Extremely fine. Rare.

701 —— Head; rev. Hands clasping Caduceus, CONCORDIA EX-
ERCITVM. Fine. Rare.

702 —— Head; rev. Fortune standing. Very fine.

703 TRAJAN, A.D., 98. Head, IMP CAES NERVA TRAJAN
OP TIM AVG. GERM. DAC.; rev. Soldier with spear and
trophy, PARTHICO PM TR COS VI PP SPQR. As it
fell from the die, and brilliant.

704 —— Head; rev. Genius with cornucopia and flowers, COS.
II. Brilliant.

705 —— Head; rev. Dacia personified, sitting on pile of shields
and arms, COS. VI. In Exrgue DAC CAP. Beautiful
and brilliant.

706 —— Head; rev. Fortune seated; in ex. FORT. RED, COS.
III. Equal to last.

707 —— Head; rev. Hercules standing front face nude, lion skin
and club, COS. IIII. As it came from the die.

Roman Imperial Coins. 57

708 TRAJAN. Head; on bust, mask and serpent; rev. Female holding double horn and scales, COS. V. Brilliant.
709 —— Head; rev. Pallas Nicephorus, with hasta, seated, COS. V. Brilliant.
710 —— Head; rev. Victory standing with palm and ? COS. V. Brilliant.
711 —— Head; rev. Emperor on Horseback, SPQR-OPTIMO-PRINCIPI. Cos. VI. Brilliant.
712 —— Head; rev. Plenty with horn and flower, Cos. II. Ex. fine.
713 —— Head; rev. The Danube, under the figure an old man reclining, DANVVIVS-COS. V. Very fine, but ancient falsification. Rare.
714 —— Head; rev. Victory crowning the Emperor; rev. Mars; rev. Peace and antelope; rev. the Emperor walking; rev. Eagle between two standards; Emperor in toga; Victory walking, with trophy, spoils, etc. As will be noticed, unusual. all fair, and some fine. 10 pieces.
715 Head; rev. Justice standing; rev. Mars standing; rev. Fortune seated; rev. Plenty standing; rev. Justice seated. All very fine. 5 pieces.
716 —— Head; rev. Temple, 3 steps, Deity within; AHMAPX. ΥΠΑΤΟ. Medallion of fine silver. Fine and rare. Tetradrachm.
717 —— Head; rev. Sheaf of wheat, ΔEMAPX. Medallion as above. Rare.
718 —— Head; rev. Half length figure of a woman wearing a basket or cistus, holding sceptre, A HMAPX ΥΠΑΤΟ. Very fine medallion, fine silver, tridrachm.
719 —— Head; rev. Eagle standing, palm and club. Same legend. Fine and rare, didrachm.
720 —— Head; rev. Eagle displayed, ΑΠΜΑΡΧ ΕΙΥΠΑΤΟ. Fine silver like the others, larger and very thick. Size 16.
721 MARCIANA (sister of Trajan). Her bust, with diadem, DIVA AVGVSTA MARCIANA; rev. Eagle *consecratio*. Very fine; one of the rarest denarii in the imperial series, valued at 100 francs, by Eckhel.
722 HADRIAN, A.D., 117. Bust, laureated and bearded, IMP CAESAR TRAIAN HADRIANVS AVG; rev. COS. II. Fortune seated, FORT. RED. Brilliant.

58   *Roman Imperial Coins.*

723 HADRIAN. Bust; rev. Concord seated. PARTHI DIVI NERVA HADRI.—TRPCOS, and in Ex. *Concord.* Brilliant.

724 —— Bust; rev. COS. II, Concord in high-back chair, patera. CONCORD. Brilliant.

725 —— Bust; rev. Vesta standing veiled, PIETAS. Cos. II. Brilliant.

726 —— Bust; rev. Fortune seated on high-back chair, patera in hand. COS. II. Brilliant.

727 —— Bust; rev. Hygeia seated feeding serpent, SALVS-AVG COS. III; and one, Fortune seated. Very fine.
2 pieces.

728 —— Head; rev. Victory carrying trophy; soldier carrying trophy; priest sacrificing; Tellus Stabil; Genius Standing FIDES PVBLICA; and Fortune seated. All fine.
6 pieces.

729 —— Head; rev. Female seated on the ground, holding in her right hand the sistrum, leaning on her left, before her, Ibis; AEGYPTOS, with rev. galley; crescent and seven stars; and the Emperor on a platform bestowing gifts. A good lot.
4 pieces.

730 —— Head; rev. Vesta walking. COS. III. Very fine. Rare.

731 —— Head; rev. Liberty seated LIB. PVB.; Concord do; Liberty with trophy; advent of the emperor, etc. Very good.
6 pieces.

732 SABINA (wife of Hadrian). Draped bust, diademed head, hair in long twist. SABINA AVGVSTA HADRIAN AVG; rev. Concord seated, CONCORDIA AVGVSTA. As perfect as when it left the die; in this condition very rare.

733 —— Head of Sabina as before; rev. Draped figure standing, holding patera and double horn of plenty, one arm resting on Cippus, CONCORDIA AVG. Very fine.

734 AELIUS (son of Annius Verus and Rupilla Faustina). Head bare, L AELIVS CAESAR; rev. Concord seated. Ex. fine.

735 ANTONINUS PIUS, A.D., 138. Head, bearded and laureated, ANTONINVS AVG, PIVS PPI PPXI; rev. Ceres before Tripod, ears of corn in hand, and in vase below, COS. IIII. Very fine.

736 —— Head; rev. Justice with scales, COS. IIII. Very fine.

Roman Imperial Coins. 59

737 A. Pius. Head; rev. Felicity standing, horn. Very fine.
738 —— Head; rev. Ceres with corn and modius, COS. IIII. Very fine.
739 —— Head; rev. Hands clasping stalks of wheat and caduceus. Very fine.
740 —— Head; rev. Peace standing; rev. Minerva standing; rev. Pomona standing. Very fine. 4 pieces.
741 —— Head; rev. Funeral pyre, 3 tiers above base, CONSECRATIO; another type (Eagle), CONSECRATIO; and thunderbolt on draped altar. Rare and good. 3 pieces.
742 FAUSTINA (the mother, wife of Ant. Pius). Head of Faustina, hair braided and jeweled, tiara on top, DIVA FAUSTINA; rev. Ceres standing, AETERNITAS. Very fine.
743 —— Head; rev. Same as last, AVGVSTAS. Very fine.
744 —— Head; rev. Vesta standing veiled. Very fine.
745 MARCUS AURELIUS, A.D., 161. Head bare of Aurelius, IMP MAVREL ANTONINVS AVG; rev. Providence standing, with globe and cornucopia. Extremely fine.
746 —— Head without beard, bare, AVRELIVS CAESAR; rev. Same as last, COS. II. Very fine.
747 —— Head *with* beard, bare; rev. Minerva with shield and spear, COS. II. Extremely fine.
748 —— Young head of Aurelius, bare; rev. Head of Ant. Pius. Very fine and rare.
749 —— Head; rev. Ceres, with corn; and denarii of Faustina (Mother), Ant. Pius, Hadrian, and Trajan. Fine lot. 10 pieces
750 FAUSTINA JUNIOR (wife of Aurelius). Head of Faustina, hair bound with strings of pearls, FAVSTINA AVGVSTA; rev. Juno standing with hasta and patera, peacock by her side, JVNONA REGINAE. Extremely fine.
751 —— Head; rev. Two nude figures on a high canopied couch, SAECVLI FELICITAS. Very fine.
752 —— Head; rev. Venus, with apple. Very fine.
753 —— Head. Veiled female beside cippus, holding bird, AETERNITAS. Very fine.
754 —— Head; rev. Concord seated. Very fine. Stained.
755 LUCIUS VERUS (associate of M. Aurelius). Head, with beard, bare; IMP L AVRE VERVS AVG; rev. Concord seated, COS II. Very fine.

60   *Roman Imperial Coins.*

756 L. Verus. Greek Medallion (Didrachm). Very fine. Rare.

757 Lucilla (wife of Verus). Head of Lucilla, with band of pearls, LVCILLA AVGVSTA; rev. Venus standing, VENVS VICTRIX. Beautiful. Rare.

758 Commodus, a. d. 180. Head of Young Commodus, bare, COM-MODO-CAES-AVG FIL; rev. Gladness personified, with palm and cornucopia, HILARITAS. Very fine.

759 —— Head, laureated and bearded; rev. MARS standing, holding branch and hasta, MART PAC-M-P-T-R-XIIII COS. Very fine.

760 —— Same; rev. Peace seated, P.M.T.R. XV. IMP. VIII COS. VI. Very fine.

761 —— Same; rev. Peace standing, patera and cornucopia, COS VI. Very fine.

762 —— Head, without beard, laureated; rev. Fortune seated, COS II. Very fine.

763 —— Head; rev. Concord seated, Justice standing, Bellona walking, Victory inscribing on tablet, Hercules standing, Mars walking, and others of the Faustina's and Aurelius's.
                                                                10 pieces

764 Crispina (wife of Commodus). Draped bust of Crispina, CRISPINA AVGVSTA; rev. Ceres standing, CERES. Ex. fine.

765 Pertinax, a. d. 193. Head, laureated and bearded, IMP CAES P. HELV-PERTIN AVG.; rev. Providence standing, in the field a star, PROVID. DEOR COS II. Extremely fine. Hardly circulated. Very rare.

766 Didit's Julianus, a. d. 193. Head, laureated and bearded, IMP CAES M DID JULIAN AVG; rev. Concord standing, holding two standards, CONCORD MILIT. Extremely fine. Equal to last. Very rare.

767 Didia Clara (daughter of Did. Julianus). Head, DIDIA CLARA AVG.; rev. Peace standing, with palm and horn of plenty. Fine, and very rare. Valued at 200 francs.

768 Pescennius Niger. Head, laureated and bearded, IMP CAES PES NIGERIVS A.; rev. Fortune standing, both hands filled, BONI EVENTVS. Very fine for this rare coin. Valued at 120 francs by Mionet.

Roman Imperial Coins. 61

769 SEPTIMUS SEVERUS, A.D. 198. Head, laureated and bearded, SEVERVS PIVS AVG.; rev. Victory erecting trophy, P.M.TR.P. XV. COS III-P.P., and one with Victory and shield. As they came from the die. 2 pieces
770 —— Head; rev. Emperor in toga, veiled, holding olive branch, FVNDATOR PACIS; and Mars with trophy, COS II. In same condition as last. 2 pieces
771 —— Head; rev. Hope walking, BONA SPES; and Plenty standing, P.M.TR.P. XIIII COS II P.P. Extremely fine. 2 pieces
772 —— Head; rev. Cybele on lion's back, INDVLGENTIA AVGG IN CATH, and Woman seated, feeding serpent, on her knee a mask, COS III. Extremely fine. 2 pieces
773 —— Head; rev. Plenty standing, and Emperor on horseback Very fine. 2 pieces
774 —— Head; rev. Victory, and one, rev. Mars. Very fine. 2 pieces
775 JULIA DOMNA (wife of Severus). Head of JVLIA PIA FELIX AVG.; rev. Diana in biga of ponies, LVNA LVCIFERA. Very fine and rare, but base silver.
776 —— Head, JVLIA AVGVSTA (same); rev. Empress before an altar sacrificing, and one, rev. Woman suckling child. (Good silver.) Very fine. 2 pieces
777 CARACALLA, A.D. 211. Head of Young Antoninus (whose name was Mar-Aur-Sev-Ant-Aug), laureated; rev. The Emperor Sept. Sev. standing, Victory in hand, and trophy and two captives, COS IIII. PART.MAX. Ex. fine. 2 pieces
778 —— Laureated, beardless head; rev. Victory passing to left, VICT. PART. MAX., and Health feeding serpent in her arms. As they came from the die. 2 pieces
779 —— Same head; rev. Victory carrying wreath; and Liberty holding hasta and cap, star in field. Splendid. 2 pieces
780 —— Same head; rev. Apollo Phœbus to left, star in field; and Emperor seated before burning altar, PONTIF TR. P X COS XII. Very fine. 2 pieces
781 —— Beardless Heads. Various reverses. No duplicates Ex. fine. 6 pieces

62   *Roman Imperial Coins.*

782 CARACALLA, A. D. 211. Head. laureated and bearded; rev. Aurora behind four horses, COS IIII.; and Mars with trophy. Extremely fine. 2 pieces.

783 —— Same; rev. Abundance standing, and Emperor walking, holding olive and sceptre. Extremely fine.
2 pieces

784 —— Same. Various reverses. Fine. 4 pieces

785 —— Head crowned, large size; Pallas Nicephorus seated, and Hygeia standing, feeding serpent. Splendid.
2 pieces

786 —— Same; rev. Peace standing. lance in hand. Ex. fine.

787 PLAUTILLA (wife of Caracalla). Head of Plautilla; rev. Head of Caracalla. Extremely fine.

788 —— Head; rev. Concord standing. Extremely fine.

789 GETA (mother of Caracalla). Head of Geta, P SEPT GETA CAES PONT; rev. Emperor holding Victory. Brilliant.

790 —— Head. Geta standing near a trophy, and Victory, with shield on base. Extremely fine. 2 pieces

791 —— Head. The Emperor sacrificing, VOTA PVBLICA, and another. Very fine. 2 pieces

792 MACRINUS, A. D. 217. Head, IMP M OPEL SEV MACRINVS AVG; rev. Young Man between two standards, FIDES MILITVM. Fine and rare.

793 DIADUMENIANUS (son of Macrinus). Head of M. OPEL. ANT. DIADVMENIANVS AVG.; rev. Young Man between three standards, PRIN JVVENTVTIS. Ex. fine and very rare.

794 ELEGABALUS, A. D. 218. Head; rev. the Emperor sacrificing, in one hand image of Baal, in the other patera; in the field the sun, SACERD-DEI-SOLIS-ELAGAB. Extremely fine. Rare.

795 —— Head, IMP CAE M. AVR. ANT. AVG. PTR.; rev. Female standing, FIDI PVBLICA. Ex. fine.

796 JULIA SOEMIAS (mother of Elagabalus). Head, JVLIA SOEMIAS AVG.; rev. Venus seated, at her knee a child: VENVS CAELESTIS. Extremely fine. Scarce.

797 —— Same; rev. Venus standing. Equally fine. Scarce.

798 JULIA MAESA (aunt of Elagabalus). Head, JVLIA MAESA AVG. ; rev. Modesty seated, PVDICITIA. Ex. fine.
799 —— Same ; rev. Priest before the altar, holding caduceus and patera, in the field star (or sun). Extremely fine.
800 —— Same ; rev. Woman standing, FECVNDITAS AVG. Fine.
801 SEVERUS ALEXANDER, A. D. 222. Laureated head of young Alexander, IMP. M. AVR. SEV. ALEXAND. AVG. ; rev. Providence standing, a globe at her feet, PROVID DEORVM, and one, rev. Health seated before a cistus, feeding serpent. As they came from the die. 2 pieces
802 —— Same ; rev. Peace standing, PAX AETERN. AVG., and Jupiter holding thunderbolt. Equal to last.
2 pieces
803 —— Same ; rev. Mars standing, and Plenty standing by a measure. Extremely fine. 2 pieces
804 —— Beardless Heads. Various reverses. Extremely fine.
6 pieces
805 —— Head, laureated and bearded ; rev. Hope standing, SPES. PVBLICA ; rev. Mars marching, MARS VLTOR. As they came from the die. 2 pieces
806 —— Same ; rev. Equity standing ; rev. the Emperor sacrificing, ANNONA AVG. Brilliant. 2 pieces
807 —— Same ; rev. Mars with trophy, and another. Brilliant.
2 pieces
808 JULIA MAMAEA (Mother of Severus). Bust of Julia, draped ; rev. Juno standing, hasta and patera; at her feet peacock, JVNO CONSERVATRIX. Brilliant.
809 —— Head ; rev. Woman leaning on cippus, in her hand caduceus. Ex. fine.
810 —— Head ; rev. Vesta standing with hasta and palladium, VESTA. Extremely fine.
811 —— Head ; rev. Venus Victrix standing with casque. Stained. Fine.
812 MAXIMINUS I., A.D. 235. Head laureated, IMP MAXIMINVS. PIVS·AVG ; rev., Peace standing, PAX AVGVSTI. Brilliant.
813 —— Duplicate. Equally fine.
814 —— Head ; rev., Victory bearing palm, VICTORIA AVG. Brilliant.

64   Roman Imperial Coins.

815 SEVERUS ALEXANDER, A..D 222. Head; rev., Loyalty between two standards, FEIDS MILITUM. Brilliant.

816 —— Head; rev., Hygeia feeding serpent, SALVS.AVGVSTI. Equally fine.

817 —— Head; rev., Providence standing, globe and horn; and soldier between standards. Ex. fine.   2 pieces.

818 GORDIANUS AFRICANUS, A.D. 237. Laureated head, IMP M. ANT. GORDIANVS AF R AVG.; rev., the Emperor with olive branch and sceptre, PMTR COS PP. Very fine and extremely rare. Valued at 100 francs.

819 GORDIANUS AFRICANUS, JR., A.D. 237. Laureated head, short beard, IMP. M. ANT GORDIANVS AFR AVG; rev., Victory passing left with palm and crown, VICTORIA AVGG. As it came from the die. Brilliant, extremely rare.

These two coins are of about equal rarity, and so fine that they would be remarkable if they belonged to the very common series of Gordian III.

820 GORDIANUS PIUS, A.D. 238. Head with radiated crown, IMP GORDIANVS PIVS FEL AVG.; rev., Hercules resting on his club, VIRTVTI AVGVSTI. Brilliant.

821 —— Head; rev., Emperor with lance and globe, COS. II. Brilliant.

822 —— Head; Gladness standing with staff and crown, LAETITIA AVG M. Brilliant.

823 —— Head; rev., Peace holding olive branch, seated; COS. II. Brilliant.

824 —— Head; rev., Justice standing, scales; Fame do with globe. Brilliant.   2 pieces.

825 —— Head; rev., Mars passing, and Loyalty standing. Extremely fine.   2 pieces.

826 —— Head; rev., Two varieties of Peace; one of Victory. Brilliant.   3 pieces.

827 —— Head; rev., Security, Fortune, Fame. All brilliant.
   3 pieces.

828 —— Head; rev., Liberality, Fame, Virtue. All brilliant.
   3 pieces.

829 —— Head; rev., Fortune, The Sun, Providence. All brilliant.   3 pieces.

830 —— Head; rev., Jove standing, thunderbolt, and Emperor sacrificing. All brilliant.   3 pieces.

Roman Imperial Coins. 65

831 GORDIANUS PIUS, A.D. 238· Head ; rev., Felicity, Liberality, Victory. Extremely fine. 3 pieces.
832 PHILIP I., A.D. 244. Head crowned, IMP M. JVL PHILIP- PVS AVG.; rev., Hygeia feeding serpent, SALVS AVG. Brilliant.
833 —— Head ; rev., Ceres standing, ANNONA. AVGG, Peace do. Brilliant. 2 pieces.
834 —— Head ; rev., Emperor seated in Curule chair, sceptre and globe ; with Equity holding Scales, and Security seated ; brilliant. 3 pieces.
835 —— Head ; rev., FIDES MILIT, FELICITAS TEMP & ROMÆ ÆTERNA. Brilliant. 3 pieces.
836 —— Head ; rev., on cippus, COS III, Emperor on horseback ; =on an Elephant=Temple, Jupiter within ; = & LAETITI. Magnificent. 4 pieces.
837 OTACILIA SEVERA (wife of Philip). Head, M. OTACIL. SEVERA—AVG ; rev., Concord seated, CONCORDIA AVGG. Brilliant.
838 —— Head ; rev., Piety standing, Juno standing, Modesty seated. Brilliant. 3 pieces.
839 PHILIP, JR. (son of Philip I.) Young head crowned M JVL PHILIPPVS CAES; rev., the Emperor with globe ;= Emperor and son seated on Curule chair, and Emperor with spear and globe. Very fine. 3 pieces.
840 TRAJANUS DECIUS, A.D. 247. Head crowned, IMP CN-M. Q TRAJANVS DECIUS AVG ; rev., Plenty with horn, ABVNDANTIA AVG. Brilliant.
841 —— Head ; rev., Emperor on horseback, and Victory with crown. Brilliant. 2 pieces.
842 —— Head ; rev., nude figure, patera, horn and modius beside standard ; and woman with dog's head on staff, DACIA (rare). Extremely fine. 2 pieces.
843 —— Head ; rev., Implements of sacrifice ; and two women with standards, PANNONIAE (rare). Extremely fine. 2 pieces.
844 —— Head ; rev., like last, except that the standards are unlike those on the other, an are carried in a different manner. Very fine and rare.
845 —— Head ; rev., Woman standing with measure and horn, and Victory passing. Extremely fine. 2 pieces.

66   *Roman Imperial Coins.*

846 ETRUSCILIA. Wife of Decius. Head of Herennia Etruscilia; rev., Woman and child standing, FECVNDITAS AVG· Brilliant.

847 —— Head; rev., Modesty seated, hasta and veil, PVDICITIA AVG. Brilliant.

848 —— Same; rev., Modesty standing. Brilliant.

849 TREBONIANUS GALLUS, A.D. 251. Head, IMP CAE C. VIB TREB GALLVS; rev., Liberty leaning on cippus, holding hasta and cap, LIBERTAS AVGG. Brilliant. Rare variety.

850 —— Head; Fame standing with globe, AETERNITAS AVG. Brilliant.

851 —— Head; rev., Happiness standing with Caduceus and horn of Plenty. Brilliant.

852 —— Head; rev., Peace holding olive branch; Piety, hands raised. Very fine. 2 pieces.

853 —— Head; rev., Juno seated, holding sceptre and ? Brilliant.

854 —— Head; rev., Apollo standing. *Apollo salutare.* Very fine.

855 VOLUSIANUS, A.D. 253. Head crowned, bearded, C. VIB VO LVSIAN AVG; rev., Mars standing, VIRTVS AVGG. Piety with uplifted hands, PIETAS AVGG. Brilliant. 2 pieces.

856 —— Head; rev., Concord standing; Peace do, hasta and olive branch, in the field a star. Extremely fine. 2 pieces.

857 —— Head; rev., Hygeia standing feeding serpent; Concord seated; and the Emperor standing. COS II. Fine. 3 pieces.

858 VALERIAN, A.D. 253. Head of C. P. VALERIANVS AVG; rev., Loyalty between two standards, FIDES MILITVM. Ex. fine.

859 —— Head; rev., Happiness standing with Caduceus and horn. Ex. fine.

860 —— Head; rev., Victory with palm, Jupiter with thunderbolt, Consecratio; and another. Very fine. 4 pieces.

861 MARINIANA (wife of Valerian). Veiled head; rev., Peacock. Rare, very good.

862 GALLIENUS, A.D. 253. Radiated head; rev., Mars standing. Ex. fine and thick.

Roman Imperial Coins.

863 GALLIENUS, A.D. 253. Head; rev., Peace standing. Briiliant.

864 —— Head; rev., Warrior, Emperor and Victory, Happiness, Piety, Providence, Rome Nicephorus, Victory, Mars, Emperor and Soldier, Hygiea, Diana Lucina, Apollo and others. No duplicates. A collection of reverses illustrative of the age of this superstitious Emperor, who thought to stay the plague by such devices. The metal base, but the *condition* of the coins all that could be desired.
20 pieces.

865 SALONINA (wife of Gallienus). Diademed head; rev., Happiness seated, FELICITAS PVBLICAS. Ex. fine.

866 —— Head; rev., Juno with patera and hasta, peacock at her feet. Brilliant.

867 —— Head; rev., Emperor and Empress joining hands, and Juno. Fine. 3 pieces.

868 VALERIANUS JR. (son of Gallienus). Head; rev., Child riding a goat, JOVI CRESCENTI; and Pontifical implements. Fine. 2 pieces.

869 POSTUMUS (Tyrant), A.D. 267. Head; rev., Moneta standing. MONETA AVG. Extremely fine, bright.

870 —— Head; rev., Providence holding hasta and flower. Fine.

871 PROBUS, A.D. 276. Marcus Aurelius Probus Augustus. Bust crowned, rich collar and breast-plate with wreath; rev., Figure leaning on a Cippus, SECVRIT-PERP., in Ex., IIIXX. Very beautiful and rare; base, but bright.
Size 16.

872 —— Duplicate. Equally fine.

873 —— Helmeted head, crowned; rev., Mars armed, passing to left, MARTI PACIF, in Exergue, OXX. Very fine; same quality of silver and size.

874 —— Head; rev., Peace standing (statue). Very fine.

875 —— Same; rev., Health standing. Very fine.

876 MAXIMIANUS, A.D. 286. Laureated head, hair and beard short; rev., Justice with drawn sword and banner, FEL ADVENT AVGG NN. Fine silver denarius.

877 CONSTANTIUS CHLORUS, A.D. 305. Laureated head; rev., four soldiers sacrificing before a Prætorian camp, VIRTVS MILITVM. Denarius of fine silver. Rare.

878 LICINIUS, A.D. 313. Head, LICINIVS JVN. NOB. C.; rev., CAESARVM—NOSTRORUM. VOT VDC, within large and small wreath of laurel. Fine silver, very rare.

68   *Roman Imperial Coins.*

879 CRISPUS, A.D. 306. Head, CRISPVS. NOB. CAES.; rev., VOT X. DOMINO NOSTRO. Fine, very rare.
A suspected coin on general principles; the existence of any genuine being doubted.

880 VALENS, A.D. 364. Head of Flavius Valens; rev., Rome Nicephorus seated. Fine silver, brilliant.

881 —— Head; rev., within laurel wreath, VOT X MVLT XX. Fine denarius.

882 HONORIUS, A.D. 395. Bust of Honorius with the Paludamentum (soldier's cloak); rev., Rome Nicephorus seated, VIRTVS ROMANORVM. Very fine.

883 —— Duplicate. Equally fine.

884 JUSTINIAN I., A.D. 527. Bust, with paludamentum and fillets, JVSTINIANOS P P AVG; rev., Monogram of Christ. Very fine, rare, Quinarius.

885 LEO III. with Constantine IV., A.D. 716; rev., Crowned head, front face, Mund and Cross, DN LE PN MYS; rev., Crowned head, star on each side, DN CON TAN TIN. Large fine silver double penny. Very rare (cost 20 francs).

886 —— Smaller; crowned head on each side. Penny. Brilliant. Extremely rare.

887 FIGURE, with Nimbus, on throne; rev., two figures standing, one holding the Labarum, the other Nimbused. Extremely fine, double penny, fine silver.

888 PERSIAN Coin; on each side, six pointed stars, unknown letters within. Drachma. Very fine.

889 OTTO. OTTO in circle. Penny.

890 COINS of the Middle Ages. Curious. 5 pieces.

ROMAN COINS.

BRASS.

[G. B., M. B., and S. B., represent in the same order, the 1st, 2d, and 3d size.]

891 POMPEY (The great, Triumvir), B.C. 49. Janus head, with portraits of Cneius and Sextus Pompey, father and son, in beaded circle; MGN; rev. prow of a galley, PIVS. M.P. Patinated and fine. " As."   Size G. B.

892 JULIUS CAESAR (Dictator), B.C. 47. Head laureated, DIVOS JVLIVS; rev. bare head of Augustus, DIVI. F. CAESAR. Fine green patination. *Very* fine and rare.   G. B.

893 AUGUSTUS, B.C. 31. Bare head of Augustus; rev. within laurel wreath DIVOS JULIVS. Patinated, fine. G. B.
894 —— Laureated head, L. DIVVS AVGVSTVS PATER; rev. thunderbolt, S.C. Patinated and very fine. M. B.
895 —— Duplicate. Equally fine. M. B.
896 —— Triplicate. Equally fine. (All beautifully patinated.) M. B.
897 —— Crowned head; rev. altar of Lyons, PROVIDENT, S.C Patinated and very fine. M. B.
898 —— Duplicate. Very *large* and fine, not patinated. Size 20
899 —— Head, DIVVS AVGVSTVS S.C.; rev. the Emperor holding olive branch and apple on curule chair, CONSENSV SENAT ET EQORDIN-PQR. Patinated and fine. M. B.
900 —— Head, IMP CAESAR DIVI F AVGVSTVS INV; rev. PONTIF MAXIM TRIBVNIT XXXIIII. Large S.C. patinated and very fine. M. B
901 —— Bare head; PONTIF MAX. TRIBVNIC-POT; rev. M AECILIVS TVLLVS III VIR. Patinated and fine. M. B.
902 —— Head, R.; rev. CASSIVS S.C. Patinated, very good, rare. M. B.
903 —— Heads of Augustus and Agrippa, IMP DIVI F PP.; rev. crocodile chained to palm tree, Col. NEM. Patinated and extra fine. M. B.
904 —— Duplicate. Patinated and very fine.
905 —— Head; rev. sacrificial implements,=Col. Nem.=thunderbolt = temple (Hexastyle), and AVGVSTVS within laurel crown. All patinated, and some rare. Very desirable.
5 pieces
906 —— Head, thunderbolt in field; rev. Rome seated; rev. eagle on globe, and of the Moneyers *Plotius*, *Nerva*, and *Agrippa*. A good lot, rather rare. 5 pieces
907 AGRIPPA (Son-in-law of Augustus). Head, M AGRIPPA L F COS III; rev. Neptune standing, with dolphin and trident. Patinated and very fine. M. B.
908 —— Duplicate. Equal to last.
909 TIBERIUS, A.D. 14. TI-CAESAR DIVI. AGG. F. AVGVST PM. S.C.; rev. Quadriga of elephants, the Emperor seated on the sacred car, THENSA, DIVO AVGVSTO SPQR. Clear and sharp generally, corroded in two places, very rare. G. B.

910 TIBERIUS, A.D. 14. Triumphal Quidriga, GERMANICVS CAESAR; rev. Germanicus standing, in R. hand a recaptured Roman eagle, SIGNIS RECEPTIS DEVICTVS GERM. S.C. In rather poor preservation, very rare. M. B.
[Struck to honor Germanicus for having recovered eagles and other ensigns lost by Varus in a battle with the Germans.]

911 —— Head of Tiberius; rev. Caduceus winged, fine. M. B.

912 DRUSUS (brother of Tiberius). Head, DRVSVS CAESAR TI AVGVSTVS F DIVI AVG.N; rev. ITER. PONTIF. TRIBVN. POTEST. S.C. Patinated and ex. fine. M. B.

913 —— Duplicate. Patinated.

914 —— Head to R., lituus, IM-NER. CLAVD CAESAR (his name was Nero Claudius Drusus); rev. within a laurel crown and inner circle, S.C. Thick coin, extremely fine, rare. G. B.

915 ANTONIA (wife of Drusus). Head, ANTONIA AVGVSTA; rev. figure standing, TI. CLAVDIVS. S.C. Very good. M. B.

916 GERMANICUS (son of Drusus and Antonia). Head, GERMANICVS CAESAR AVG. F DIVI AVG. N.; rev. TI. CLAVDIVS CAES. S.C. Patinated and very fine. M. B.

917 —— Head; rev. within wreath of laurel and circle. S.C. Very fine. S. B.

918 CALIGULA, A.D. 37 (Divi Aug. Pronepos). Head of Caius Caesar Aug.; rev. VESTA, Vesta seated. Ordinary. M. B.

919 —— Cap of Liberty, S.C., C CAESAR DIVI AVG PRON AVG.; rev. RCC. around, COSTERT, PON IN. TR.P. Beautifully patinated, and sharp as when struck. S. B.

920 CLAUDIUS, A.D. 41 (Ti. Claud.). Head of Tiberius, TI. CLAVDIVS CAES AVG. P. M. TR - P. IMP.; rev. Hope standing, SPES. AVGVSTA. S.C. Patinated, moderately fine and very rare. G. B.

921 —— Head, leg, same; rev. Liberty standing, LIBERTAS AVG. S.C. Patinated and fine. M. B.

922 —— Head; rev. Constancy and rev. Clemency. Fine.
2 pieces

923 —— Head, in field, star; rev. bull butting, AYTOKPA. Struck at Alexandria; rev. extremely fine, rare. M. B.

924 —— Head, COS XXXIIII; rev. within wreath S.C. Fine.
M. B.

Roman Brass Coins.

925 CLAUDIUS, A.D. 41. Modius on tripod; rev. S.C. Beautifully patinated. S. B. 2 pieces

926 NERO, A.D. 54. Head laureated, to R., NERO CLAVD CAESAR AVG GERM-T.M. IM PPP; rev. temple of Janus shut, TERRA MARIQV PARTHVS JANVM CLVSIT. S.C. Perfectly patinated and *extremely* fine. G. B.

927 —— Duplicate. Patinated and very fine. G. B.

928 —— Head laureated to *left*, NERO CAESAR AVG GERM M.F.T; rev. like last. Beautifully patinated and very fine. M. B.

929 —— Head to r. Equal in every respect. M. B.

930 —— Head to r.: rev. Victory holding globe bearing SPQR. S.C. Patinated and very fine. M. B.

931 —— Duplicate. Same in all respects.

932 —— Same. Without patination, very fine. 2 pieces

933 —— Head with turreted crown; rev. GLORIA. AVGVSTA. on rev. Rome seated and Alexandrian. M. B. 4 pieces

934 —— Head to r. and l., NERO CAESAR AVG IMP; rev. actor's stage (?), supporting vase and civic crown, underneath mask? CERO VI NO ROMA CON. Patinated and very fine. S. B. 2 pieces

935 —— Duplicate of last, with another—Eagle on altar; rev. olive tree, S.C. Patinated and fine. S. B. 2 pieces

936 GALBA, A.D. 68. Head of Sergius Sulpicius Galba; rev. Liberty standing, LIBERTAS. S.C. Patinated, rare. M. B.

937 VESPASIAN, A.D. 69. Head of Flavian Vespasian, radiated crown; rev. Ceres standing, CERES AVGVSTA S.C. Perfectly patinated and extremly fine. M. B.

938 —— Head laureated; rev. Hercules standing, S.C. Equal to last.

939 —— Same; rev. Eagle on globe. Patinated and fine.

940 —— Same; rev. FELICITAS-PVBLICA=LAETITIA do= Æ QVITAS AVGVSTI. M. B. 3 pieces

941 —— Head of Vespasian; rev. head of Isis (Alexandrian), and •one with Victory inscribing on a shield hung to a tree. JOYDAI VESHASIANOC. Extremely rare coins. S. B. 2 pieces

942 —— Others relating to the Conquest of Judea. Patinated and fine. S. B. 3 pieces

72   *Roman Brass Coins.*

943 Titus, A.D. 79. Head of Titus; rev. Peace standing. Fine.
M. B.

944 —— Vase or measure on 3 feet; rev. in laurel crown, S.C. Very fine.   S. B.

945 Domitian, A.D. 81. Head of Imp. Caesar Domit. Aug. Germ. Cos, etc., etc.; rev. Mars standing, VIRTVTI AVGVSTI. S.C, Beautiful green patination. Ex. fine.   M. B.

946 —— Laureated head of Domitian; rev. temple with 5 pillars, AVGVSTA, S.C. Perfectly patinated. Very fine. M. B.

947 —— Head to left, IMP CAESAR DIVI VESP. F. DOMITIAN. AVG.; rev. Mars standing, TRP COS VII DES VIII P.P. Perfectly patinated and beautiful.   M. B.

948 —— Head; rev. Minerva standing. Equal to last. M. B.

949 —— Head; rev. Fortune standing. The same. M. B.

950 —— Head; rev. Moneta standing. Patinated and fine. M.B.

951 —— Head; Mars resting, VIRTVTI AVGVSTA, Mars charging, S.C. = and Victory and trophy. All patinated.
3 pieces

952 —— Imp DOMIT AVG GERM. S.C.; rev. in beaded circle, rhinoceros; olive tree, ILIVMI. 100; rev. in circle of *two* snakes with heads and tails joined, two horse shoes; head of Domitian; rev. bundle of wheat and poppies, S.C.; green as emeralds and perfect as when struck.
S. B. 3 pieces

953 Nerva, A.D. 96. Head laureated of Marcus Cocceius Nerva; rev. Liberty standing, LIBERTAS PVBLICAS. S.C. Patinated and very fine. Rare.   G. B.

954 —— Same, except size. Patinated and extra fine. M. B.

955 —— Head; rev. Fortune standing. Pea green, ex. fine. M. B.

956 Trajan, A.D. 98. Head of Marcus Ulpius Trajanus without beard, laureated; rev. horseman riding at full gallop over prostrate enemy, S.P.Q.R. OPTIMO. PRINCIPI. S.C. Perfectly patinated and ex. fine.   G. B.

957 —— Head; rev. Abundance before Modius, with poppy and two ears of corn. Legend, same as last. Very fine. G. B.

958 —— Head; rev. Victory with shield, SPQR. Cos. IIII. Pat'd and ex. fine.   M. B.

959 —— Head; rev. Victory before trophy, S.P.Q.R. OP-PR., etc. Patinated and ex. fine.   M. B.

Roman Brass Coins. 73

TRAJAN. Head; rev. Fortune standing. Patinated and fine. M.B.
—— Head; rev. man and yoke of oxen, " Col. Berytus," obv. patinated and fine; rev. slightly rubbed. Very rare. M. B.
—— Head; rev. Victory. Red and green patination. Fine.
2 pieces
—— Head; rev. Fortune seated, with cornucopia and rudder. Patinated pea green. Very fine and rare. S. B.
—— Old bearded head; rev. club; rev. wild boar; rev. wolf; rev. rhinoceros. Perfectly patinated in different colors. Little gems. S. B. 4 pieces

HADRIAN, A.D. 117. Head of Nerva Trajanus Hadrianus; rev Felicity standing. Beautiful light blue patination and fine. Rare. G. B.
—— Rev. the river Nile personified, recumbent. Struck at Alexandria. Rather poor, rare. G. B.
—— Laureated head; rev. Peace standing. Fine. G. B.
—— Rev. Rome seated; Galley; Victory; and Health sacrificing. G. B. 4 pieces
—— Head, HADRIANVS AVGVSTVS; rev. Pallas, shield, and uplifted spear. Beautifully patinated. Very fine. M. B.
—— Head; rev. Equity seated, scales and cornucopia. Same condition. M. B.
—— Head; rev. Galley, FELICITATI AVG S.C. Same condition. M. B.
—— Head; rev. Nile on the ground, Ibis on Cippus, AEGYPTOS, S.C. Perfectly patinated, sage green. Extremely fine. Rare. M. B.
—— Head; rev. Peace, with cornu copia and olive branch. Patinated. Fine. M. B.
—— Head; rev. Pegasus; rev. Liberty standing. Patinated. M. B. 2 pieces
—— Head; rev. Ceres standing, holding corn and plough, on the ground Modius, with wheat heads and poppy. Another of the "Annona" type, the Modius very high, also with corn and poppies. Well patinated and sharp.
2 pieces.

SABINA (wife of Hadrian). Her head; rev. the Empress seated. Well patinated; obv. fine. Rare. M. B.

AELIUS, CAESAR. Head; rev. the Emperor and Aelius standing, CONCORDIA AVGG. Only fair. G. B

Roman Brass Coins.

978 ANTONINUS PIUS, A.D., 138. Head of Antoninus; rev. two cornu copiæ, with children, TEMPORVM FELICITAS. Fine and rare. G. B.

979 —— Head; rev. Emperor seated, INDVLGENTIA, AVG. S.C. Fine. G. B.

980 —— Head, ANTONINVS AVG. PIVS, S.P.P.; rev. Peace standing, with olive branch and cornu copia. Beautifully patinated, sage green. Ex. fine. M. B.

981 —— Head; rev. Ceres standing, cornu copia, and both hands filled with flowers, fruit and corn. Equal to last. Rare. M. B.

982 —— Head; rev. Woman standing, FECVNDITY. In the same splendid condition, emerald green. M. B.

983 —— Head; rev. Peace standing, PAX AVG. Same condition. M.B.

984 —— Head; rev. Justice seated, JVSTITIA; rev. Pallas with, uplifted arm, and Ceres seated, ANNONA AVG. Fine, well patinated. M. B. 3 pieces

985 —— Head *crowned*; rev. Justice with scales. Patinated, sharp and fine. M. B.

986 —— Head; rev. Emperor sacrificing, VOTA SVSCEPTA S.C. Perectly patinated, and fine. M. B.

987 —— Laureated head; rev. Elephant. Patinated and fine. Rare. M. B.

988 —— Bust, ANTOININOC; rev. Peace standing beside a lamb, ΓAZA. Thick barbarous coin. Fine. G. B.

989 —— Head; rev. Felicity; rev. The Emperor in toga. Very fine. 2 pieces

990 —— Head; rev. Honor, Piety, Mars. Good coins. G. B. 3 pieces

991 FAUSTINA (wife of Antoninus). Head of of Galeria Faustina; rev. the Emperor sacrificing, PIETAS, S.C. Well patinated and fine. G. B.

992 —— Head; rev. Ceres holding torch, and armful of fruit and branches. Perfectly patinated. Fine. Rare. G. B.

993 —— Head; rev. figure bending over a burning altar, with patera In hand, CONSECRATIO. Well patinated and fine. M. B.

994 —— Head, DIVA FAVSTINA; rev. AETERNITAS; and rev. the Emperor standing with lance and globe. Patinated and fine. M.B. 2 pieces

Roman Brass Coins. 75

995 FAUSTINA Head of Faustina veiled; rev. Sacrifice. G. B
996 MARCUS AURELIUS, A.D., 161 (adopted son of Ant. Pius).
— Bare head, AVRELIVS CAESAR AVG; rev. Pallas, shield and uplifted lance, S.C., sage green. Very beautiful, one of the gems of the collection. G. B.
997 — Same head; rev. Ceres standing before altar. Patinated and ex. fine.
998 — Laureated head; rev. Hygiea feeding serpent, SALVTI. Very fine. G. B.
999 — Same; rev. Mars with spear, and on shield S.C. Patinated and ex. fine. M. B.
1000 — Bust, with back and breast plate, radiated crown; rev. Peace, with wreath and olive branch; and Fortune seated. Patinated, and fine. M. B. 2 pieces
1001 — Head; rev. Consecratio types with eagles. Patinated. Rare. G. B. 2 pieces
1002 — Head; rev. Victory, palm and crown; and Virtue. Fine. G. B. 2 pieces
1003 — Head; rev. Mars standing; rev. Equity seated. Patinated. Fine. G. B. 2 pieces
1004 — Head, radiated crown; rev. Captives and trophy, DE. GERM. Laureated head, rev. Victory with crown and palm; beautiful green. Fine and rare. M. B. 2 pieces
1005 — Radiated head; rev. Mars standing; and "Concordia," M. B. 2 pieces
1006 FAUSTINA (wife of Aurelius). Head of Annia Faustina; rev. Ceres seated, with torch and two ears of corn. Patinated and fine. Rare. G. B.
1007 — Head; rev. "Ilium" (in Greek letters); rev. Juno standing; rev. Ceres standing. Well patinated and rare. M. B. 3 pieces
1008 LUCIUS VERUS (colleague of Aurelius). Head; rev. the two Emperors joining hands, CONCORDIA AVGC. Not patinated, but a good coin. G. B.
1009 LUCILLA (wife of Verus). Head; rev. Venus seated. Patinated, and fine. M.B.
1010 — Head; rev. Ceres seated, ANNONA AVG, etc. Patinated. G. B.
1011 COMMODUS. A.D. 180. Head bare; rev. Security standing with hasta and Caduceus, COSII. Patinated and fine. G. B.

1012 COMMODUS. Head laureated, rev. Ceres standing to r., Lares to l., Modius with five ears of wheat, ANNONA AVG. Fine and rare. G. B.
1013 —— Head; rev. Valor seated, VIRTVS AVG IMPIII COS II. Fine and very large, medallion size. Size 22
1014 —— Head; rev. Gladness standing with palm and cornu copia. Fine. G. B.
1015 —— Head; rev. Implements of worship, and Mars with trophy and lance. Patinated and fine. M. B. 2 pieces
1016 CRISPINA (wife of Commodus). Head of Crispina; rev. Venus holding apple. Beautifully patinated. Extremely fine. M B.
1017 —— Head; rev. Juno standing. Fine. M. B.
1018 PERTINAX, A.D. 193. Laureated head to r., ins. illegible; rev. temple with pointed gable, twenty-two columns shown (one side and end given), above, IOMH, below, COL HE=preservation, especially reverse, very good. Of course, rare. M. B.
1019 SEPTIMUS SEVERUS, A.D., 193. Head, IMP SEV PERT AVG; rev. the Emperor bearing Victory (Nicephorus) and spear, VIRTVS AVG S.C. Very fine. G. B.
1020 —— Same; rev. the Emperor on horseback, attendant on foot leading horse, ADVENTVS AVG. Very good. G. B.
1021 JULIA DOMNA (wife of Severus). Head, JVLIA AVGVSTA; rev. Juno with peacock, S.C. Blue patination. Rare. G. B.
1022 —— Head, JVLIA PIA FELIX AVG (Domna); rev. Felicity standing. Greenish brown patination. Rare. M. B.
1023 CARACALLA, A.D., 211. Head, M ANTONINVS PIVS AVG Caracalla; rev. Venus Victrix with helmet, shield, and spear, holding Victory, VENVS VICTRIX. S. B.
1024 —— Head; rev. Eagle, in beak, wreath, DEMARX. Potin.
1025 GETA (brother of Caracalla). Head of Septimus Geta; rev. Rome Nicephorus seated, VIRTVS AVGVSTA. Patination perfect, sage green. Fine and rare. M. B.
1026 —— Geta with his father, Sept. Severus; their heads; and one of his mother, J. Domna, rev. temple. Rare. S. B. 2 pieces

1027 MACRINUS, A.D., 217. Head; rev. Security leaning on a
Cippus, in r. hand hasta. Rare. *Good.* M. B

1028 DIADAMENIANUS (brother of Macrinus). Head of M. Opel
Sev. Macrinus; rev. in olive wreath, S C. Very rare. Fine.
S. B.
[So rare as to be valued for S. 600 francs, for brass, 40].

1029 ELAGABALUS, A.D. 218. Head of M. Aur. Ant. Aug. Elagabalus; rev. Victory hurrying with palm and civic crown,
VICTORIA ANTONINI, AVG. S. C. Fine. G. B.

1030 —— His coins in a suite of 4 sizes, with good reverses,
from, G. B. to the smallest—one Colonial of Berytus, with
temple of Neptune. 4 pieces

1031 ANNIA FAUSTINA (third wife of Elagabalus). Head of Faustina, ANIA FAVSTINA AVGVSTA; rev. the Emperor
and Empress standing joining hands, CONCORDIA. Very
fine. M. B.
[This coin is *rare to excess;* the estimated value by the highest
authorities is 600 francs. It is genuine and warranted.]

1032 JULIA SOEMIAS (Mother of Elagabalus). Head; rev. the
Empress seated, child at her knee, VENVS CAELESTIS.
S.C. Fine and rare. G. B.

1033 SEVERUS ALEXANDER, A.D. 222. Beardless head to r.,
laureated, IMP. ALEXANDER PIVS AVG.; rev. Apollo
with whip, head radiated, r. hand raised, TRPXII, COSIII
Perfectly and beautifully patinated. Extremely fine. G. B.

1034 —— Same; rev. Ceres standing, Modius and Corn. Equal
to last. G. B.

1035 —— Same; rev.'s of last two, Remarkably fine.
G. B. 2 pieces

1036 —— Head with spiked crown; rev. Ceres standing. Patinated and fine. M. B.

1037 —— Laureated head; rev. Hope standing; rev. Apollo
standing; rev. Jupiter, Tonans standing. All very fine.
G. B. 3 pieces

1038 JULIA MAMÆA (mother of Alexander). Head of Julia Mamœa,
Augusta; rev. Venus seated, hasta and child in hand,
VENVS FELIX. Fine turquoise blue; as fine as the day
it was struck. G. B.

1039 —— Same; rev. Felicity with Caduceus, leaning on a short
column, FELICITAI PVBLICA. Patinated and very fine.
G. B.

1040 JULIA MAMÆA Same; rev. Venus standing, child and hast in hands. VENVS FELIX and VENERI FELICI. Patinated, very fine. G. B. 2 pieces

1041 —— Same; rev. turreted head; rev. Venus Victrix. G. B. 2 pieces

1042 MAXIMINUS. A.D. 235. Laureated head. MAXIMINVS PIVS AVGVSTVS; rev. Victory holding crown and palm. VICTORIA GERMANICA. Fine green patina. One of the finest in the series. G. B.

1043 —— Head; rev. Peace, standing. PAX AVGVSTI S.C. Very fine. G. B.

1044 —— Head; rev. Health feeding serpent. SALVS, etc. Very fine. G. B.

1045 MAXIMUS. (Son of Maximinus). Young head bare; rev. the prince near two standards, with baton and spear. PRINCIPI JVVENTVTIS. S.C. Brown patination. Extremely fine. G. B.

1046 BALBINUS. A.D. 237. Head laureated. IMP CAES D. CAEL. BALBINVS AVG.; rev. Security standing, with hasta and Caduceus. Beautiful sage-green patination. Ex. fine, rare. G. B.

1047 GORDIANUS PIUS. A.D. 238. Head laureated. IMP CAES M. ANT. GORDIANVS AVG.; rev. Peace standing. PAX AVGVST. S.C. Pea-green, and beautiful; a gem. G. B.

1048 —— Head; rev. Apollo? standing with globe; head radinated. AETERNITATI AVG. S.C. Equal to last. G. B.

1049 —— Head; rev. Liberty standing, with hasta and cap. Pale green patination. Extremely fine. G. B.

1050 —— Head; rev. Felicity, with Caduceus and cornucopia. FELICI-TEMPOR. Very dark green, very fine. G. B.

1051 —— Head; rev. "Laetitia;" "Jovi-Stator;" "Jovi Conservator," with thunderbolt and hasta, to L., child. All very fine. G. B. 3 pieces

1052 —— Head; rev. Victory with palm, and Genius between two standards. Extremely fine coins. G. B. 2 pieces

1053 —— Head; rev. Concord, seated. Extremely fine, and perfectly patinated. M. B.

1054 CORDIANVS PIVS. Coin of Viminiacvm, Mœsia. Head of Gordianus rev. woman between lion and bull. PMS COL VII. ANI. (See Humphrey's Manual, p. 310.) Patinated, and fine. A rare coin. G. B.

1055 —— Coin of the Colony, "Julia," head ; rev. temple of Astarte, the goddess within ; her bust full face, with horns. COL JVL AVG FEL BER. Patinated, and very fine. M. B.
Simply rare 8, or highest degree. See Calmet "Astarte."

1056 —— Another coin of "Berytus;" rev. Neptune, nude, with trident in one hand, in the other a dolphin. One of Egypt, in billon, rev. eagle ; and others. Very rare lot, different sizes. 5 pieces

1057 SABINA TRANQUILLINA (wife of Gordian) ; obv. bust of Sabina; rev. the emperor and empress joining hands. CONCORDIA AVGG. Small size, base metal.
I do not like the coin, yet it may be genuine. It is as rare as any in the Catalogue ; marked by Eckhel 600 francs.

1058 PHILIP (Arabian). A.D. 244. Head of M. Julius Philippus Aug.; rev. Security with Cornucopia and Caduceus. Patinated and very fine. G. B.

1059 —— Head ; rev. 4 standards surmounted by human heads ; lion and horned head of Isis. FIDES EXERCITVS-SC. Patinated and very fine, rare. G. B.

1060 —— Head ; rev. man on elephant's back. AEQVITAS AVG. Patinated and fine, rare. G. B.

1061 —— Head ; rev. the emperor royally dressed, sitting on curule chair, holding sceptre and globe. Extremely fine. G. B.

1062 —— Head ; rev. soldier standing, Fortune seated, Liberality standing, and Ceres standing. All fine. G. B. 4 pieces

1063 —— Head ; rev. column with ins. relating to secular games, and Security standing. Beautifully patinated, very fine. M. B. 2 pieces

1064 OTACILIA SEVERA (wife of Philip I.) Head of Marcia O t Sev.; rev. the empress seated. PVDICITIA AVG. Very fine. G. B.

1065 —— Head ; rev. Concord seated, and duplicate of last Very fine. 2 pieces

1066 —— Colonial of Berytus (in Syria). Full length figure of Astarte in her temple. Well patinated, and when cleaned will be very fine. Rare. M. B.

1067 PHILIP II. (Son of the Arab). Laureated head of Caesar; rev. the emperor and Caesar on a double curule chair. LIBERALITAS AVGG. Bright pea-green, one of the beauties of the series. G. B.

1068 —— Head. AYTOKK M IOYAI ΦIVIΠΠOC CEB.; rev. woman sitting on a pile of rocks, eagle standing on her arm, horse galloping at her feet, her head turreted. ΦA CAMO-CA DKM. The coin fine and remarkable, having the appearance of a medallion. Size 21

1069 —— Head; rev. the prince with spear and ball. *Extremely fine.* G. B.

1070 TRAJANUS DECIUS. A.D. 249. Head of Q. Trajanus Decius; rev. Dacia (or the province personified), standing with the dog-headed standard, DACIA. Very fine, rare. G. B.

1071 —— Duplicate, perfectly patinated, fine but irregular shape. G. B.

1072 —— Beautifully patinated little S. B. 2 pieces

1073 TREBONIANUS GALLUS. A.D. 251. Head; rev. soldier standing. VIRTVS AVC. Very good. G. B.

1074 —— Head; rev. Mars in his temple. Patinated. G. B.

1075 —— Colonial of Alexandria (Troas), head; rev. eagle standing on forepart of an ox. Col. TROAS. Very fine. S. B.

1076 VALERIAN. A.D. 253. Head of Cn. Pub. Licin. Val. radiated; rev. Hercules erecting a trophy. Large and unusual coin. G. B.

1077 —— Head, laureated; rev. Apollo Phœbus. ORIENS AVG. G. B.

1078 —— The same; rev. Providence standing. Thick, square coin, perfectly patinated and fine. G. B.

1079 GALLIENUS. A.D. 253. Head; rev. warrior standing. VIRTVS AVGVSTVS. S.C. Thick, square coin, fine and rare. G. B.

1080 SALONINA. Wife of Gallican; bust of Salonina, diademed head; rev. the goddess Astarte holding cross, Victory standing on a column placing a crown on her head. COL JVL. AVG FEL. BER. Patinated and ex. fine. G. B

The Phoenician Astarte was sometimes represented with the cross, but not at all relative to Christianity. See account of her worship, by Calmet. This coin was struck at Berytus, (Beyrout),

Roman Brass Coins.

1081 VICTORINUS. (Tyrant). A.D. 268. Helmeted head, VICTORINVS; rev. bird standing. Perfectly patinated, and fine thick coin, very rare. M. B.

1082 CLAUDIUS GOTHICUS. A.D. 268. Laureated head. AVT ΚΛΑVΔ; rev. eagle with wreath, head, r. and l. Billon. Extremely fine. 2 pieces

1083 —— Head in radiated crown. CONSECRATIO. Three types. Ex. fine. 3 pieces

1084 —— Same; rev. Equity, Jupiter Tonans, Liberty, Security, etc. Ex. fine. 6 pieces

1085 —— Laureated head; rev. lion and eagle. Beautiful. 3 pieces

1086 QUINTILLUS. (Brother of the Goth). A.D. 270. Radiated head; rev. woman holding anchor and wreath. Ex. fine. S. B.

1087 AURELIAN. A.D. 270. Bust, laureated with cuirass and paludamentum; rev. the emperor and empress joining hands, in field, radiated head of Apollo Phœbus, (Sun), CONCORDIA. Perfectly patinated, dark green, and fine. Extremely rare. M. B., size 19

1088 —— Another of this rare type. Splendid.

1089 —— Greek legend; rev. eagle between standards, thick coin billon. Ex. fine. 2 pieces

1090 —— Bust, radiate and laureate, with paludamentum and cuirass; rev. Valor presenting Victory to the emperor, and other equally fine reverses, all patinated and splendid. S. B., 4 pieces

1091 SEVERINA. (Wife of Aurelian). Diademed head of Sev. Augusta; rev. Juno, hasta patera and peacock. JVNO REGINA. Patination, fawn color or pale green. Beautiful and rare. M. B

1091a —— Duplicate, dark green. Equally fine. M. B.

1092 VABALATHUS HERMAS. (Son of Zenobia). A.D. 264. Head of Vab.; rev. head of Aurelian. Extremely fine and rare. S. B.

1093 TETRICUS. A.D. 273. (C. Pesuvius, the younger, his father was P. Pesuvius). Head; rev. Mars, standing. VIRTVS AVG. Ex. fine. S. B.

1094 TACITUS. A.D. 275. Head; rev. Providence, at her feet, globe. Beautiful. S. B.

1095 FLORIANUS. A.D. 276. Radiated bust, cuirass and paludamentum; rev. Hygiea feeding serpent. SALVS AVG. Perfect. S. B.

The paludamentum was a sort of cloak worn by soldiers, often over their cuirass, (breast-plate).

1096 PROBUS. A.D. 276. Bust with radiated crown, cuirass, and palud., selection of reverses. Eg. quadriga, the sun as charioteer; emperor on horseback; temple, etc. Extremely fine and interesting. S. B., 10 pieces

1097 CARUS. A.D. 282. Bust as before; rev. Jupiter Nicephorus standing, at his feet, eagle. JOVI VICTORI. Ex. fine. S. B

1097a —— Same. Hope standing. SPES PVBLICA. Ex. fine. S. B.

1098 DIOCLETIAN. A.D. 285. Head, laureate bearded; rev. Moneta standing with scales and cornucopiæ. SACRA MONETA AVGG ET CAESS. NOSTR., and two others. *Largest size*, or M. B., rare. 3 pieces

1099 —— Same; rev. Ceres standing, both hands filled. SALVS. AVGG. ET. CAESS FELIX. ART. Brilliant, (tin surface), as from the mint. Largest size.

1100 —— Bust, radiate crown, cuir. and pal.; reverses, various; interesting for the numbers and abb's in exergues. Patinated, and fine. S. B., 8 pieces

1101 MAXIMIANUS HERCULES. A.D. 286. Head laureated; rev. Ceres standing. (See des., same rev. on coin of Diocletian). Brilliant, largest size.

1102 —— Same; rev. Pallas standing in helmet and toga, at her feet, owl. FELIX ADVENT AVGG NM. Brilliant, same size.

1103 —— Same; rev. Moneta. (See Diocletian). Genius standing, GENIO POPVLI ROMANI. Jupiter standing, and others, of the largest size and very fine. 5 pieces

1104 —— Head, radiate, cuir. and palud.; rev. Jupiter Tonans, with eagle; soldiers with Victory on their joined hands; Votive, etc. Patinated, green as emeralds, and perfect as when struck. S. B. 8 pieces

1105 —— Head, veiled; rev. eagle; rev. lion, MEMORIAE ETERNAE. Gems. 2 pieces

1105a —— Head, various reverses. S. B. 10 pcs

Roman Brass Coins.

1106 SEVERUS II. A.D. 305. (Flavius Val. Sev.) Head laureate; rev. Ceres standing, both hands full. (See former des.) Largest size. Brilliant.

1107 CONSTANTIUS CHLORUS. A.D. 305. Laureated and bearded head; rev. Moneta standing, cornucopia and scales. (See Diocletian). First size, patinated and ex. fine.

1108 —— Same; rev. "Genio Populi Romani." & "Fides Militum," v. fine, first size.   2 pieces

1109 —— Head, reverses varied, different sizes, green and beautiful.   6 pieces

1110 HELENA. (First wife of Chlorus). Diademed head of Flav.. Julia Helena Augusta, (Draped bust); rev. Security with olive branch, below, Crescent, SECVRITAS REIPVBLICAE. Perfectly patinated, and extremely fine, rare. S. B.

1111 —— Same; rev. Peace standing. PAX PVBLICA. Equal to last.

1112 GALERIUS MAXIMIANUS II. A.D. 305. Bust with spiked crown; rev. "Vot XX." In olive wreath, patinated, and fine, rare.

1113 MAXENTIUS, A. D. 306. Head Laureate of Marcus Aur. Val. Maxentius; rev. Temple, within, Deity sitting, CONSERVA VRBS; and one, Dioscurii standing, AETERNITAS, etc. Very fine. 1st size.   2 pieces

1114 —— Same; rev. Victory writing on shield, on the ground Captive; Dioscuri beside their coursers; Apollo standing; and "Votive." Different sizes. Ex. fine.   5 pieces

1115 LICINIUS 1ST, A. D. 313. Laureated Head; rev. Jupiter Nicephorus, at his feet eagle, JOVI. CONSERVATORI; another, Jupiter, at his feet crown. Variety. Very fine.   4 pieces

THE LOWER ROMAN EMPIRE.

(So called from the time of Constantine the Great.)

1116 CONSTANTINE 1ST (the Great), A. D. 306. Flavius Valerius Constantinus Maximus Aug., Bust, laureate, with cuirass and paludamentum; rev. Apollo standing, SOLI INVICTI; rev. Temple, PROVIDENTIAE AVGG; rev.

Emperor transfixing fallen horseman, FEL TEMP REPARATIO; rev. Two Soldiers with a single standard, GLORIA EXERCITVS; do. with two do.; same leg; VOTXX, etc., with laurel crown; and others, all patinated and fine; the varieties not described equal to those that are. Truly an admirable lot of 20 pieces

1117 —— Repeated as nearly as possible. No duplicates.
15 pieces

1118 —— Similar lot. 10 pieces

1119 FAUSTA (Flavia Maxima, second wife of Constantine). Bust of Fausta, hair coifed with pearls, in four rolls and knot; rev. Hope standing, with two children in arms, in Exerg. Crescent, SPES REPVBLICAE N IV. Perfectly beautiful. S. B.

1120 CRISPUS (son of Constantine). Bust of Fl. Jul. Crispus, laureate, sceptre and olive branch; rev. Jupiter Nicephorus; rev. Temple, above, star; rev. VOTX in wreath. All patinated, and as fine as possible. 3 pieces

1121 HELENA (wife of Crispus). Diadem'd Bust, necklace and earrings; rev. Emperor on prow, with captive, FEL TEMP REPARATIO. Not fine, but well preserved, and rare. S. B.

1122 HANNIBALLIANUS (Flav. Claudius, nephew and son-in-law of Constantine the Great), A. D. 335. Bust of Hannibalian bare, paludamentum and cuirass, FL. HANNIBALIANO. REGI; rev. River God seated on ground, holding sceptre in both hands, beside him a reed and urn overturned, from which water is flowing, in Exergue CONS. Patinated and in *perfect* preservation. S. B.

[The title of "King," which had been assumed by no Roman prince since the expulsion of the Tarquins, was given Hannibalian by Constantine, whose daughter he married, and who made him Governor of Pontus and Armenia. This coin is held by all authorities to be most rare and remarkable. It will be found wrapped as it was purchased, with the mark, "50 Francs."]

1123 CONSTANTINE II. (son of Constantine 1st and Fausta), A. D. 337. Head, laureate; rev. Monogram of Christ, and others.
S. B. 4 pieces

1124 CONSTANS (Flav. Jul.), A. D. 337. Bust, laureated, with paludamentum; rev. Eagle on rock, holding wreath, to left star, VICTORIAE DD AVGG (bright green, and very fine), and another. S. B. 2 pieces

Roman Brass, Lower Empire. 85

1125 NEPOTIAN (Flav. Nep. Cons. Aug., nephew of Cons. the Great), A. D. 350. Head, bound with chain; rev. Rome, Nicephorus seated, SECVRITAS PVBLICA. Patinated. Fine. M. B. Size 16
[This piece is extremely rare. The value is 100 francs, by the same authority that places Magnentius at 2, and Decentius at 8 francs.]

1126 MAGNENTIUS, A. D. 350. Bust, laureate, in palud.; rev. Horseman charging, under the horse wild boar? Very fine.

1127 DECENTIUS (brother of Magnentius), A.D. 351. Bust as before; rev. Two Victories holding tablet, ins. VOT V MVLT.X., and around ANNONA AVG ET. CEAS.

1128 CONSTANTIUS II. (son of Constantine and Fausta), A. D. 350. Bust, laureated, sometimes with spiked crown, paludamentum and cuirass; rev. Emperor on prow, holding the sacred banner, globe, and eagle—by his side captive—GLORIA ROMANORVM; Emp. transfixing horse and rider, FEL TEMP, etc. ——, leading captive, two trees to left, etc. Patinated. Fine. 6 pieces

1129 —— Similar lot. Very fine. 8 pieces

1130 JULIAN III. (Apostate), A. D. 361. Bust; rev. in laurel wreath VOTX MVLT XX, etc. Perfectly patinated, and fine. S. B.

1131 —— Bust; rev. Julian striking down horse and rider. Ex. fine. S. B.

1132 HELENA (wife of Julian Apostate). Flavia Julia Helena Aug. Head, 3 rows pearls, FL.I. HELENA; rev. Emperor and captive. Rare. S. B.

1133 JOVIAN, A. D. 364. Bust of Flavius Jovianus, fillet palud. and cuirass; rev. VOT. V MVLT.X., wreath. Patinated and fine. Rare. S. B.

1134 VALENTINIANUS, A. D. 364. Same as last. FL VALENTINIANVS AVG; rev. Victory with palm and civic crown; temple and sun; the Emperor holding Labarum, dragging captive by hair. Patinated and extremely fine. 3 pieces

1135 —— Similar. Equally fine. 3 pieces

1136 —— Head, with helmet, cuirass, and palud.; rev. Emperor in galley, man steering, and two others. 3 pieces

[The coins of Valentinianus in the last three lots cost, in gold, 48 francs, and they were purchased in Paris long since. This hint is to remind purchasers that they are *fine* and *valuable*, though for rarity, not to be compared with hundreds of others in the Catalogue.]

86   *Roman Brass, Lower Empire.*

1137 VALENS, A. D. 364. Bust of Flavius Valens in the same style as last; rev. Soldier, with labarum, forcing captive to right; Victory passing to left. Varieties. Very fine.
    4 pieces

1138 —— Same; rev. Victory passing with palm and crown.
    4 pieces

1139 GRATIAN, A. D. 367. Bust as before, FL. GRATIANVS AVG; rev. Soldier with labarum and captive, GLORIA ROMANORVM; Emperor helmeted, lance, globe and cross, CONCORDIA. Ex. fine.
    2 pieces

1140 —— Helmeted Head; rev. Emperor in galley, and another.
    2 pieces

1141 THEODOSIUS I., A. D. 379. Bust filleted, paludamentum and cuirass; rev. Emp. with labarum and ball, one foot on captive; Emperor in galley, and others.
    4 pieces

1142 —— Bust ——; rev. VOTXV. MVLTXX., and another. Ex. fine.
    2 pieces

1143 ARCADIUS A. D. 395. Bust, FL ARCADIVS AVG; rev. Two Victories with crowns, VICTORIAE AVGG. Ex. fine. A gem.
    S. B.

1144 —— Head; rev. Emperor with standard and globe, and others.
    3 pieces

1145 HONORIUS, A. D. 395. Head; rev. Emperor crowned by Victory. Deep sage green. Extremely fine.
    S. B.

[The succession virtually ends here; and, indeed, it is customary for collectors to bring their lists to a conclusion with the reign of Theodosius I., in whose time the division of the Empire took place.]

1146 CONSTANTINE III. (Tyrant), A. D. 407. Bust, full face, mund and cross, DN CONSTANP; rev. G. cross and star. (Rare. 40 francs.) Very good.
    M. B.

1147 CONSTANS II. (son of last). Bust as before, DN CONSTANP PAV; rev. XX above +, in Ex ROM. Patinated and extremely fine and rare (40 frs.)
    M. B.

1148 —— Bust, full face, crowned; rev. $^{ANNO}M^{III}_{C}$. Not fine, but ex. rare.
    G. B.

1149 CONSTANTIUS III., PATRICIUS, A. D. 421. Bust, in profile, to right, in paludamentum, CONSTANTIVS PP AVG.; rev. M with + between * *, in Ex. CON. *Extremely rare.*
    M. B.

Roman Brass, Lower Empire. 87

1150 ANASTASIUS, A. D. 491. (See account of his restoration of the large brass Sestertius.) Profile Bust to right, DN AN-ASTASIVS PP AVG; rev., within wreath, large M and cross between * *, in Ex CON. Rather poor, but distinct. G. B. Size 21

1151 —— Same; rev., in hollow, large K *, to left cross NI. Patinated. Fine and rare. S. B. Size 13

1152 JUSTINUS I. (Aug.), A. D. 518. Bust; rev. $^A_N I^X_{IIII}$; another, A *. S. B. 2 pieces

1153 JUSTINIANUS I., A. D. 527. Full face crowned Bust, in paludamentum and cuirass, DN IVSTINIANVS PP AVG; rev., within wreath, large M with + —. to left, anno to right x: in exergue CON. Extremely fine. G. B. Size 26

1154 —— Duplicate. Very fine. Nearly equal to last. G. B. Size 23
[Having been without G B so long, these noble Romans rather overdid the new enterprise.]

1155 —— Same; rev. * I * inclosed in wreath. Patinated and fine. Rare. S. B. 2 pieces

1156 —— Repetition of last. Equally fine. 2 pieces

1157 —— Bust, in profile, to right; rev. K to left *, to right +; all within wreath. Patinated and extremely fine. (Very rare type.) M. B.

1158 MAURICIUS, A.D., 582, Maur. Tiberius Aug. Bust, full face, with globe and cross; rev. Within wreath, large M with cross. to l ANNO. to r. X. II. I., in Exergue CON. patinated, black and fine (12 francs). G. B.

1159 —— Same; rev. XX with cross, in Ex. ROM. Green. Very fine. S. B.

1160 —— Same; rev. Different numerals, in Ex. CON. Fine. Very rare. S. B.

88   *Roman Brass, Lower Empire.*

1161 HERACLIUS II. (Constantius), A.D., 641. Heads of Heraclius and Tiberius; rev. XX. in Ex. ROMA, patinated and fine (6 francs).   S. B., 2 pieces.

1162 JUSTINIANUS II (Rhinotmetus), A.D., 685. Bust to r in paludamentum and cuirass, head filleted; rev. large M. with cross between two stars, all within laurel wreath, most beautifully patinated, and extremely fine; so rare that the large brass is not mentioned by Mionet or Eckhel. Small B. 12 francs. A very valuable coin.
G. B., Size 21

1163 LEO III (Isaurus). A.D., 741. Heads of Leo III & IIII. and Constantine VI.; rev. Large K. to l. ANNO, in Ex. ROM. Patinated and fine.   2 pieces.

1164 COINS of this Period, unclassified. The Cross and other religious symbols prevalent.   S. B., 12 pieces.

1165 CONSTANTINOPLIS and Urbs Roma; rev. Victory on prow, and the she wolf suckling Romulus and Remus. Patinated and fine, with others of the same character.   24 pieces.

1166 MISCELLANEOUS. A few of which are good coins. 20 pieces.

SPINTRÆ TESSERA, ETC.

1167 TIBERIUS CAESAR. Obv. Two figures in lascivious postures; rev. Within wreath and beaded circle, 111. Patinated and fine.   C., Size 13

1168 —— Same; Figures in different postures; rev. 1111. Equally fine.

(Found in the island of Caprea and *rare.* Joseph Addison, in his tour through Italy, in the years 1701, 1702 and 1703, came across some of these little spintræ, and remarks concerning them: "The bear on one side some lewd invention of that hellish society, and on the other the number of the medal. Those I have conversed with about it are of opinion they were made to ridicule Tiberius, though I cannot but think they were stamped by his order.")

1169 TESSERA, used in the Phallique and Bacchic mysteries, (little tokens in lead). Very free; from Pompeii. 4 pieces.

1170 —— Used probably as tokens in connection with games and shows of animals.   25 pieces.

1171 —— Similar, representations of animals, etc. 25 pieces.

1172 —— Same.   25 pieces.

Spintræ Tessera, etc.

1173	TESSERA. Same.	25 pieces
1174	—— Same.	25 pieces.
1175	—— Same.	25 pieces.

(These Tessera are about the size of the Denarius. They are all made of lead and stamped on both sides with images of men, animals, trees, implements used in worship, initial letters, monograms, etc., etc. They were dug up on the site of the ancient city of Pompeii, and are unquestionably antique.)

1176	—— Same.	25 pieces.
1177	—— Same.	50 pieces
1178	—— Same.	50 pieces.
1179	—— Same.	100 pieces.
1180	COLORED GLASS from the same locality, fragments of rare and beautiful vases, craters, patera, etc. Selected.	10 pieces.
1181	—— Same, including beads, ring, stones, etc.	10 pieces.
1182	—— Same.	25 pieces.
1183	—— Same. Miscellaneous colored enamels.	25 pieces.
1184	—— Same.	25 pieces.
1185	—— Same. Large number; the lot.	——
1186	LACHRYMATORIES. Beautifully iradescent, from same and other localities. Perfect or nearly so.	4 pieces.
1187	Same. Unusual forms.	2 pieces.
1188	Same.	4 pieces.
1189	PATERA, diameter 6 inches, Irised glass. Perfect.	
1190	BRONZES, from same locality. MIRRORS, one nearly perfect.	2 pieces.
1191	—— Fragments of mirrors, bails, handles, etc.	6 pieces.
1192	FIBULA. Very perfect and elaborate. A remarkably fine antique.	
1193	LARES (bronze), of Egyptian origin. Perfect and fine, 3 inches high.	2 pieces.
1194	YOUTH Crowned with Wreath of Roses, in his hand a patera. Fine Figure. Bronze.	
1195	ATLAS. Fine, nude, 4 inches tall, perfect, and of magnificent work; perhaps "Cinque Cento." A gem.	
1196	TERRA COTTA LAMPS. Nearly perfect.	2 pieces.
1197	—— With figure of a dog and letters. Remarkable and fine.	
1198	—— With ornamental top, large size. Perfect and fine.	

1199 COTTA LAMPS. With symbolical figures. Imperfect. 3 pieces.
1200 —— Vases, small size. Plain. 2 pieces
1201 —— Bottles with long, slim necks, different sizes. 3 pieces.
1202 —— Others, various forms. All perfect. 4 pieces.
1203 EGYPTIAN ICUNCULÆ or Lares. Figure on Wood, face red, the Hieralpha on each side, and net behind, painted all over with hieroglyphics. Perfect. Rare and fine.
Height, 8 inches.
1204 —— Terra Cotta. Quite similar to last. Height, 5 inches.
1205 —— Deep blue porcelain, foot gone. Height, 5 inches.
1206 —— Same. Remarkably fine.
1207 —— Same. Various sizes. 3 pieces.
1208 —— Painted Terra Cotta. Remarkable form. Perfect.
1209 ANTIQUE WEIGHTS, used by druggists, one with silver triangle inserted. Small bronze. 2 pieces.
1210 TRIAL Impressions, or Artist's proofs of heads, one struck over a large coin of Agrigentum in Sicily, showing the original stamp; they show the form of the punch, and are deeply sunk into the metal. Thoroughly and beautifully patinated. Very fine and valuable. Size 21. 2 pieces.

MODERN COINS AND MEDALS.

Silver Coins.

Bohemia. Half Crown of Rudolf II., 1598. Obv., bust; rev., double eagle crowned. Rubbed. Rare.
——— Crown of Matthias, 1614. Very good and rare.
Bremen. Thaler of the City, 1753. Obv., shield supported by two lions; rev., same as 1211. Extra fine.
Brunswick. Bell Dollar of 1643. Obv., bust of Augustus in mail; rev., a bell, M. VII. B. 13. Rare and fine.
——— Crown of 1662. Obv., arms on a shield with five crests; rev., wild man and tree. Rubbed. Rare.
——— Same, except date, 1715; and finer. Rare.
——— Obv., broad crown of Christian Ind, 1663; rev., within a wreath of laurel, horse galloping. A little rubbed, still fine. Very scarce.
Denmark. Crown of Fred. III., 1656. Obv., crowned bust, long hair; rev., arms of Denmark surrounded by eleven other coats of arms under one crown. Extremely fine and beautiful crown. Rare.
——— Crown of Christian VII., with his monogram crowned, 1777. Fine.
Frankfort. Thaler of 1860. Obv., bust of a lady; rev., eagle. Very fine. [Known as the Rothschild Thaler.]
Holland. Fine Ducatoon (Crown) of 1784. Nearly uncirculated. Scarce.
Lubeck. 32 Shilling (⅔ Crown) of 1797. Very fine. Scarce.
Nuremberg. Fine Crown of 1754. Obv., bust; rev., the City. Rare.
Poland. ⅔ Crown of Augustus, 1705. Obv., bust in full dress; rev., two coats of arms. Nearly uncirculated. Rare.
Sweden. Crown (very broad) of Gustavus Adolphus, 1617. Obv., his bust in profile. sceptre and mund. Inscription in two circles; rev., the Saviour standing. Fine. Rare.
——— Half Crown of Christina, 1656. Obv., bust, ¾ face; rev., like last. Fine and rare.
——— Two Mark (⅓ Crown) of Charles XI., 1688. Very fine.

92 *Modern Coins and Medals.*

1227 STOLBERG. Crown of Wolfgang George, 1625. Obv., stag; rev., coat-of-arms. Rubbed. Broad crown. Rare.

1228 RATISBON. Crown of 1757. Franciscus, D.G., etc. X Mark. Rubbed. Scarce.

1229 WOLFGANG. Cardinal in 1728, Duke of Poland, etc., etc. Fine Crown. Three coat-of-arms under a cardinal's hat. Almost uncirculated. Rare.

1230 FERDINAND II., Archduke of Austria, 1624. Obv., his bust laureated; rev., fine coat-of-arms. Nearly uncirculated. Crown. Scarce.

1231 LEOPOLD. Archduke of Austria, 1629. Obv., profile bust; rev., coat-of-arms. Very fine crown. Scarce.

1232 REPUBLIC OF FRANCE, 1848. Five francs. Very fine.

1233 EMPIRE OF MEXICO, 1823. Obv., bust of Iturbide (Augustus); rev., eagle on cactus. Very fine dollar. Scarce.

1234 SIERRA LEONE (Africa) Company's Dollar, 1791. Obv., lion; rev., two hands clasping. Nearly proof. Rare.

1235 SCOTLAND. Dollar (full crown) of Mary Stuart and Henry Darnley, 1566. Obv., arms of Scotland; rev., a palm (or yew) tree; to left, as countermark, a thistle. The legend EXVRGAT DEVS DISSIPENT INIMCT. In very good preservation. Rare.

1236 ENGLAND. Half Crown of Anna; under the bust of the queen, VIGO, 1703. Nearly uncirculated. Rare.

1237 —— Dollar of the "Bank of England." Obv., bust of George III.; rev., Britannia seated within the garter. 1804. Fine.

1238 —— Crown of George III.; rev., St. George and Dragon, with the great artist, *Pistrucci's* name below. Splendid. Nearly proof. Rare.

1239 —— Rupee of Victoria. For India. Struck in 1862. Very fine.

1240 GEORGE IV. ⅔ Crown of Brunswick, 1828. Circulated.

SILVER MEDALS.

1241 GUSTAVUS ADOLPHUS, Sweden. Medal Crown, 1632. Obv., bust, royally dressed and laureated; rev., arms of Sweden. Extremely fine. Nearly uncirculated. Rare.

1242 —— Bust, as before, within an oval, garnished with flowers; rev., hand holding a sword, encircled by a civic

Modern Coins and Medals. 93

crown between branches of laurel and palm; above, Hebrew inscription and rays; around, long inscription in two circles, record of his birth and death. Fine proof.
Size 27.

1243 CHARLES XI., Sweden, and Ulrich Eleonora, his wife. Their busts conjoined; rev., three figures standing. FIDEI AC PACIS A LUMNUS, 1680. Lettered edge. Extremely rare medal, in fine condition. The field burnished after striking. Size 30.

1244 CHARLES XII., Sweden. On the conclusion of a treaty of peace at Breslau, 1709. Obv., bare bust; rev., lighted candle between palms on the top of a high column, against which a lion resting one paw, the other holding a sword. Fine. Uncirculated medal. Size 24.

1245 PEACE OF WESTPHALIA. Memorial Medal, 1648. Obv., caduceus and laurel twigs held by two clasped hands; the inscription around, and in five lines below; rev., Saint, holding sword and book; the legend arranged as before. A splendid proof medal. Very beautiful and rare. Size 33.

1246 GEORGE I., England. Memorial of the War with Spain, 1718. Obv., bust of the King of England; rev., amid heaps of arms, a naval column. In exergue, CLASSE HISP DELETA ANDORAS SICILIÆ, 1718. Fine and rare. Size 27.

1247 FREDERIC THE GREAT, Prussia. On Peace with Austria, 1757. Obv., bust; rev., Peace crowning trophy of arms. Extremely fine. Size 25.

1248 MARTIN LUTHER. Jubilee Medal. Obv., bust of Dr. Luther; rev., kneeling figure with cross and chalice in one hand, and open book in the other. IN MEMOR-JVBIL. SEC-LVTHER. The date found in the tall letters on obverse, 1717. Fine proof impression. Rare. Size 27.

1249 MEMORIAL OF THE PEACE OF RYSWICK, 1697. Obv., Peace standing; rev., strong military station, an angel flying over it. Very fine. Size 22.

1250 NAPOLEON BONAPARTE. Egyptian Campaign. AN. 7 Rep. Obv., bust in the Egyptian Costume; rev., crocodile chained to a palm tree. Denon Direxit. Extra fine.
Size 21.

Modern Coins and Medals.

1251 PEACE OF FRANKFORT, 1755. Obv., Female with Prussian shield sacrificing; rev., eagle bearing label, 1555; above, a globe, on which GERMANIA. Extra fine. Size 22

1252 REFORMATION Memorial Medal of Stolberg. Obv., a stag; rev., in exergue, AM REFORMATIONS, FESTE DE 31 October, 1817. Fine Proof. Size 18.

1253 CITY OF BASLE. Medal, with view of the town : rev., Circle of nine shields. Fine. Size 17

1254 TEMPERANCE MEDAL. Father Matthew Total Abstinence Pledge; with loop. Fine proof. Size 16

1255 MEDAL in Memory of the Alliance of the French and Piedmont Armies, Milan, 5th June, 1859. "Aux Blesses et Malades de l'armie," etc., etc. Size 20

1256 PRIZE MEDAL. Bruce Castle on the principal side. Fine. Size 16

BRONZE MEDALS.

1257 CATHEDRAL, Lincoln. Founded, 1085 ; burnt, 1141 ; often rebuilt, 1195–1250. Obv., exterior view ; rev., interior. Fine proof, by J. WIENER, Brussels. Size 34

1258 ———— Notre Dame, Paris. Same series. Fine proof. "

1259 ———— St. Marks, Venice. Same. Fine proof. "

1260 ———— Milan. Same. Fine proof. "

1261 CONVENT Batalha, Portugal. Same series ; exterior and interior of the Convent, with inscription in exergue. Fine proof. Size 34

1262 FREDERICK THE GREAT. Young bust ; rev., his statue (equestrian) on a monument. Splendid medal, by *Loos*. Fine proof. Size 30

1263 LOUIS PHILIPPE, of France. Obv., his bust, by *Petit* ; rev., ins. in 18 lines. Splendid proof. Size 30

1264 NICHOLAS I., Russia. Obv., his bust (by *Loos*) ; rev., legend in a wreath of laurel. Splendid proof, rare. Size 22

1265 REFORMATION MEDAL, to commemorate the third centenial festival of its celebration, June 25th, 1830. Obv., Dr. Martin Luther and Philip Melancthon standing beside an altar and open book ; rev. scene in Angsburg, Anno, 1530 ; twelve figures done in a wonderful manner by Loos and *Pfuffer*. Splendid proof. Size 26

Modern Coins and Medals. 95

1266 FRENCH "Dix Centimes," satirizing L. Napoleon. The Emperor's head incased in a Prussian helmet, the eagle on the reverse transformed into an owl. Done with great ingenuity and effect.
1267 ———— The head gear, cossack.
1268 ———— The Emperor smoking a German pipe.
1269 ———— Different.
1270 ———— Another variety.
1271 ———— Another.
1272 MEDAL to commemorate the celebration of the anniversary of American Independence in Stuttgart, July 4, 1873. Obv., the Town Hall, ERINNERUNG AN STUTTGART, LIEDERHALLE, 4 July, 1873; rev., American eagle and shield. DECLARATION OF INDEPENDENCE, 1776. With loop, tin.   Size 20

(Undoubtedly very rare, and being struck exclusively for the use of Americans on that occasion, not likely to become otherwise than rare and valuable.)

ADDENDA.

PAPAL COINS.

GOLD.

1 DOUBLE DOPPIO. Obv., St. Peter, seated on a cloud, APOSTOLOR PRINCEPS, Shield bearing a cardinal's hat, P. 60 (60 pauls); rev., lily of Bologna, 1777. Intrinsic value, 6.65 gold. A very beautiful coin, and scarce.
2 DOUBLE DOPPIO of Pius VI., 1787; rev., two shields, BONONIA DOCET. Equally fine.
3 ———— Duplicate, except date.
4 HALF DOPPIO (15 pauls). Same type as No. 1.
5 ———— Duplicate.
6 ———— Triplicate.

SILVER.

7 SCUDO. Sede Vacante MDCCCXXIII. Good, rare.
8 HALF SCUDO (50 baiocchi); obv., head of Gregory XVI.; rev., St. Romvaldus at his devotions, 1834. Fine.

Papal Coins.

9 TWENTY baiocchi. Pius IX. Very fine.

10 TEN baiocchi. Obv., arms; rev., AAA FFF restitutum commerc. Poor.

11 to 13 FIVE and three baiocchi. Poor. 3 pieces

14 to 20 FIVE and three baiocchi, with a Mortuary coin without date. All silver. 7 pieces

21 TWENTY baiocchi. Obv., arms, 1745; rev., St. Martin dividing his cloak with a beggar. Poor. Rare.

22 FIVE Pauls, Tuscany, 1778 (about 60 cents). Obv., head, Leopold, etc.; rev., arms. Fair.

23 THIRTY baiocchi. Sede Vacante, 1830. Obv., Holy Ghost descending (Dove); rev., arms, cock crowing, etc. Pierced. Very rare.

24 to 33 PAULS. Interesting variety; several 10 baiocchi coins.

KNIGHTS OF MALTA.

SILVER.

34 EMANUEL PINTO, 1761. 30-tari piece (crown). Obv., The Good Shepherd, NON SURREXIT MAJOR T. XXX; rev., arms of the order. Very fine and rare.

35 EMANUEL DE ROHAN. 20-tari piece. Obv., bust of the G. M.; rev. arms, 1796. Obv., slightly rubbed; rev., fine. Rare.

36 EMANUEL PINTO. 15-tari piece (half crown), 1769. Same type as 34. Good and very rare.

37 ———— 15 tari; as last ex., date, 1756. Equally good.

38 EMANUEL ROHAN. 15-tari piece, 1781; obv., bust; rev., crowned eagle covered by arms, crowned. Good and very rare.

39 FRANCIS XIMENA DE TEXADA. Bust; rev., arms, 1774. I. S. (Scudo). Fair, rare.

40 EMANUEL ROHAN. Scudo, 1776. Obv., mailed bust; rev., same as 38. Fine and rare.

41 ———— Scudo, 1796. Obv., bust; rev., coat-of-arms. Fine, rare.

42 ———— Six-tari piece (quarter-dollar). Obv., arm of the G. M.; rev., TVI in wreath of laurel and palm, 1776. Good and rare.

43 ———— Similar (six-tari), 1780.

Silver Coins. 97

E PINTO. (Four-tari.) Rev., arms. Good and
ilar (four-tari), bust facing left. Rubbed, rare.
E ROHAN. Four-tari, 1776. Wreath, with flowers.
od, rare.
ne, ex., date 1779. Fair.
E PINTO. Two-tari piece. Obv., shield, with 5 cres-
ev., cross. Fine and rare.
EXADA. Obv., shield, with castle; rev., cross,
n angles. Rare.
E ROHAN. Two-tari piece. Obv., arms; rev.,
te 1779 in angles. Fine and rare.
i and half-tari. Very rare.   3 pieces

ILVER COINS OF SICILY.

I. Crown (120 granas). Obv., coat-of-arms;
er god and volcano, 1749. Good.
Rep. Napolitana." Obv., liberty standing with
fasces; rev., " Anno Septimo della Liberty, Car-
ici." Very good and rare.
oachim Murat. "Gioacchino Napol. Re delle
i." Bare bust; rev., Dodici Carlini, 1810. Ex-
fine, hardly circulated, very rare.
ECE. Charles III., 1735 (60 granas). Rev., cross.
re.
granas). Same type as 52. 1736.
·dinand, 1796. Obv., bust; rev., eagle, " Hispan
Fair, rare.
rlino Sci). Half-crown, companion to 53. Fair.
PIECE. Charles III. Obv., bust; rev., cross.
e, rare.
plicate. Poor.
PIECE (quar.-dol.) Ferdinand. Rev., as last.
'IECE. Charles III. Rev., eagle. Fine, rare.
· Rev., the golden fleece, dates from 1692 to
Ordinary.   5 pieces
DINAND IV., 1796. 20 granas (about 18 cents).
ist; rev., crown.   2 pieces
844. 20 granas. Very fine, scarce.

98   *Silver Coins.*

71 and 72 Tari, or 10 granas. Charles II., 1688. Poor.
2 pieces

73 —— of Ferd. IV. Rev., cross. Good.

74 to 86 Tari and half-tari, from 1798 to 1846. No duplicates.
13 pieces

87 to 89 Two-Tari Pieces, one rare; viz.: obv., globe surmounted by a fasces and cornucopia, above them a crown, 1680. Fair.
3 pieces

SPANISH SILVER.

90 to 93 Small Coins, 8th and 16th dollars, one of the former and three of the latter. One fine.
4 pieces

FRENCH SILVER.

94 to 99 Coins of Napoleon, Charles X., and Louis Phillippe; one of the latter counterfeit. Intrinsic value of the six pieces, about 40 cents. Several rare and fine.
6 pieces

AUSTRIA, LOMBARDY, AND SARDINIA.

100 to 103 Small Coins of Charles VI., Napoleon, and Vic. Amadeus.
6 pieces

DANISH SILVER.

104 to 109 Base Coins of Fred. IV., Fred. V., Christian VII., etc.
6 pieces

MEXICAN SILVER.

110 and 111 Republic, 1832, 1843. Eighth dol.
2 pieces

MISCELLANEOUS SILVER AND BASE.

112 to 118 Maltese, 1-tari; Sicily, 1 carlini; Sardinia, ½ franc; Papal, 5 baiocchi, etc.
7 pieces

ENGLISH SILVER.

119 Crown of George III., by Pistrucchi, 1819. Good.
120 Crown of George IV., by same. 1821. Good.
121 Half Crown of George IV. Rev., "Britanniarum," etc. Fine.

Copper Coins.

122	HALF CROWN of George IV. Collar of Order of the Garter, etc.	
123 to 128	SHILLINGS of George III., George IV., and Victoria.	6 pieces
129 to 139	SIXPENCE and fourpence.	11 pieces
140 to 146	THREEPENCE and smaller.	7 "
147 to 150	OTHERS. Similar.	4 "

COPPER COINS.

A collection in wrappers, labeled and valuable, quite as much for the care and exactness with which this has been done as on any other account.

151 to 154	SICILIAN (Neapolitan) Ten and eight tornesi of Ferd. IV. and Murat.	4 pieces
155 to 159	——— Eight and six tornesi, Ferd. IV.	5 "
160 to 165	——— Five, four, and three tornesi, Ferd. IV.	6 pieces
166 to 172	——— Three, two, and one tornesi, Ferd. IV.	7 pieces
173 to 186	——— One and one-half, one, and one-half tornesi.	14 pieces
187 to 191	NEAPOLITAN, 1793 to 1806. Six, five, and four tornesi.	5 pieces
192 to 197	MALTESE Coins of Emanuel Pinto and Emanuel Rohan, from 1747 to 1778. Varieties, rare.	6 pieces
198 to 203	PAPAL Coins. "Two baiocchi," from Pius VII. to Pius IX.	6 pieces
204 to 211	OTHER Papal Coins. Baiocchi and half baiocchi.	8 pieces
212 to 214	LOMBARDO Italian Coins; Napoleon 3 and 1 centesimi.	4 pieces
215 to 219	SARDINIA and Parma, 5 to 1 centesimi.	5 "
220 to 222	PORTUGUESE and Brazilian Coins, from 40 to 10 reis. Varieties.	6 pieces
223 to 228	BELGIAN COINS.	6 pieces.
229 to 232	FRENCH COINS, Louis XVI., Republic, Napoleon III.	8 pieces.
233 to 238	Another lot. Similar.	8 "
239 to 247	Similar.	9 "
28 and 249	GENEVESE Coins.	2 "

Copper Coins.

Base Silver Coins.

250 to 259   Hamburg.   Three towered castle, from 1738 to 1790. Small coins.   10 pieces.
260 to 271   Mecklenburg Schwerin.   Small coins.   12 "
272 and 273   Bavarian (Groschen).   Max. Jos. and quarter stiver.   2 pieces.
274 to 277   Dutch Coins.   Utrecht, Frankfort, etc.   4 "
278 to 283   Palatine.   24 and 48 einen thaler (lion).   Wurtemberg, Lubee, etc.   6 pieces.
284 to 287   Hesse, etc.   12 einen thaler, etc.   4 "
288 to 299   Danish Coins.   24 to 2 skill.   12 "
300 and 301   Schleswig Holstein.   5 skill.   2 "

COPPER COINS.

302 to 307   English.   Pennies of George III. and Victoria.   6 pieces.
308 to 318   ———— George III., George IV. and Victoria. Half-pennies, farthings and half-farthings.   11 pieces.
319 to 322   Lower Canada and Nova Scotia.   Penny and half-penny.   4 pieces
323   Upper Canada and other Provinces.   12 "
324   Similar.
325   Same.
326   French Coins.   Some provincial.   8 pieces
327   Russian Coins.   Fine lot.   3 "
328   Roman   "   "   8 "
329   Belgian, Sicilian, etc.   12 "
330   Miscellaneous Coppers.   50 "
331   Similar lot.   50 "
332   Similar lot.   Smaller coins.   50 "
333   Another lot.   100 "
334   American Shin-Plasters and Half-cents.   32 "
335   ———— Tokens.   Randall & Co., Baltimore.   Tom Thumb weight, 15 lbs., and California counter.   Fine and rare.   4 pieces
336   Other Tokens.   Foreign.   Fine.   3 "
337 to 351   Pendant Medalets.   Most of them brass, in brilliant proof condition, from one and a half to half-inch in diameter.   French, English, and Papal.   14 "

352 BASE Coins. All containing silver, except two Spanish counterfeits. Small. — 66 "
353 FINE Silver Coins. English 4d., 3d. Sardinian 5 granas, etc. Av. half-dime size. — 19 pieces
354 —— Six Carlini. Napolitan Rep. Anno Septimo. Equal to 62 cents.
355 —— 20 baiocchi. Uncirculated. — 2 pieces
356 —— Shillings of George III. Rubbed. — 3 "
357 —— Sicilian Coins (intrinsic value of the lot, one dollar.) — 8 pieces
358 ANCIENT Coins. Small brass, and illegible. — 12 "
359 —— Greek and Roman. Brass. Poor. — 7 "
360 —— Second brass of Augustus and some of Constantine Chlorus, Constantine II. and Maximinus. A fine lot. — 5 pieces
361 —— MISCELLANEOUS. 1 curious medal. — 4 "

ORIENTAL COINS.

362 YIRMILEK. Egypt. 20 piastres. Gold. Fine.
363 —— Turkey. " " " Proof.
364 —— Ottoman " " " Pierced
365 ONLIK. Egypt. 10 " " Fine.
366 —— Turkey. " " " Proof.
367 —— Ottoman. " " " Fine.
368 BESHLIK. Turkey. 5 " " Proof.
369 —— " " " " "
370 —— Ottoman " " " Fine.
371 GOLD Coins. Half-dollar size. Thin. — 4 pieces
372 SILVER Dollar of Turkey. Obv., the *Toghra* of the Sultan; rev., place, etc., mintage. Edge engrailed. Uncirculated. (20 piastres.)
373 —— Half-dollar. Same. Uncirculated. (10 piastres.)
374 —— Quarter-dollar. Same. Very fine. (5 piastres.)
375 —— Eight " Uncirculated. (2½ piastres.)
376 —— One Piastre. "
377 —— Half-piastre. "
378 —— (44 per cent., fine) Piece of six, three, and one and a half Piastre, and a single para. Uncirculated set. 5 pieces
379 —— (lower quality), large and small pieces. Never in circulation. — 6 pieces
380 OTTOMAN Empire. Different alloys. Base silver. 15 pieces
381 INDIA. Rupees. Fine silver. — 2 "
382 TURKISH Coppers. — 6 "
383 CHINESE Cash. — 6 "

MISCELLANEOUS COINS.

SILVER.

384 AMERICAN Dollar of 1794. Poor. Rare.
385 TRANSYLVANIA Dollar of 1596. Bust of Sigismund, holding sceptre. Fine, rare.
386 PAPAL Coin. Intrinsic value, 40 cents. Clem. XII. Poor.
387 RUSSIAN Coin. Zarma Katharine, 1788. Quarter Dollar. Fine.
388 SALZBURG. 3 Groshen, 1691; rev., St. Rupert. Uncirculated. Rare.
389 BURGUNDY. Third crown, no date. Mailed horse and rider in circle of 17 shields. Maximilian standing on rev. Splendid. Rare.
390 BATAVIA. Quarter Guilder, 1802. Ship. Extra fine.
391 EPISCOPACY of Olmutz VI., Groschen, 1675. Uncirculated. Rare.
392 EPISCOPACY of Treves, 1774. 10 krs. Ex. fine.
393 MEDALET in honor of Maximilian, Imp. of Germany, Olmutz, 1762. Quarter-dollar size. Uncirculated.
394 MEDALET. MANET, and 3 coins. Fine lot. 4 pieces
395 POLISH. John Casmir. No date, on rough planchet. Little worn. Rare. Franc size.

COPPER.

396 SWEDISH Coins of Necessity. Daler's of Baron Goerck. No duplicates, ordinary. 7 pieces
397 PAPAL three baiocchi, 1849. Fine.
398 AUCTORI Plebis. Rev. harp, and rev. plain. Faint impressions, not uncirculated. Rare. 2 pieces
399 ANCIENT first brass of Maximinus Pius. Rev., Victory. Perfectly patinated, cracked. Fine and rare.
400 ANCIENT. 1st size, same. Rev., "Pax." Fine, rare.
401 ANCIENT. 1st size, Philip II. Rev., elephant carrying the Prince. Very good.
402 ANCIENT of Valens, A.D. 378. Small coins. 2 pieces
403 ANCIENT Greek of Demetrius Polyorates (the city taker). Rev., Neptune, standing, and Egyptian; rev., tripod. Poor. 2 pieces
404 DENARIUS of Trojan. A very fine coin, broken in two pieces.

Miscellaneous Coins.

405	FRANKLIN Cents. Ordinary.	10 pieces
406	MASSACHUSETTS Cents, 1787–8. Fair and poor.	10 "
407	CONNECTICUT Cents. Rare varieties, rather poor.	10 "
408	VERMONT Cents. Several very rare, rather poor.	10 "
409	NEW JERSEY Cents. Varieties, rather poor.	10 "
410	NEW YORK Cents. Including Talbot, Allan, and Lee, and Georgius Triumpho. Rather poor, but scarce.	5 pieces
411	WASHINGTON Cents, double head. Independence and North Wales. Poor.	3 pieces.
412	COLONIAL, of the foregoing varieties. All in rather poor condition.	25 pieces
413	NORTH AMERICAN tokens. Wood's token, Colonial, etc. ; all American. Poor.	75 pieces
414	SHIPS, Colonies, and Commerce. Rev., a ship with American flag; in ex. W. & B., N. Y. (Wright & Bale.) Good, rare.	
415	——— Others with and without W. & B.; with American flag and British flag; with Buchanan and Harrison tokens, and miscellaneous coppers. None strictly fine.	75 pieces
416	OLD store cards, copper, size of the old cent. Some rare, one a cow "A friend to the Constitution," on the rev. of Gibb's card, etc., etc. Some poor, but generally a good lot; many duplicates.	118 pieces
417	SHIN-PLASTERS of 1837. Very good lot.	272 pieces
418	COPPERHEADS, copper and brass. Fine.	52 pieces
419	UNITED STATES Cents and Half Cents. All old, many early dates, not the worst of which is a "93" Liberty cap, broken die. While there are good pieces among them, taken as a whole, it is a poor lot.	200 pieces
420	ENGLISH trade tokens, half-penny size. A choice collection, strictly uncirculated and bright; rare varieties of fine execution, not to be excelled for quality.	30 pieces
421	——— Penny size; Druid's head, Welsh feather, Cornish penny, British Copper Co., penny token 1811 (Geo. III.), etc. Fair.	10 pieces
422	ENGLISH Pennies, with some for British Provinces, e. g., Nova Scotia, Canada, Demerara, Ceylon, Barbados, etc. Fair.	12 pieces
423	ENGLISH Pennies and Half-pennies, with some for Canada and other provinces; a great variety, from William and Mary to Victoria. Generally in very good condition.	25 pieces

Miscellaneous Coins.

424 St. Helena. Vale-Mitad, Catalonia, Chili, 1 Macuta (Africa), Due Baiocchi (Roman Rep), Obsidional Anvers, 1814, large Reessean, 1681, twopenny piece of Geo. III., and others equally fine and scarce. All strictly fine; large size. 20 pieces

425 Isle of Guernsey, Jersey, Man, Gibraltar, with bright Canadian half-pennies. A choice lot. 10 pieces

426 Demerara. Catalonia, E. I. Co., Malacca (rev., rooster), Buenos Ayres, and a variety of uncirculated English, French, and Belgian coins in sets. Fine lot. 22 pieces

427 Model English coins, medals of royal children, weights, etc. Fine. 10 pieces

428 Paine hanging; open book, labeled, The Wrongs of Man, 1793, with Wm. Till's card (dealer in coins, etc.) Both rare, with trade half-pennies. 25 pieces

429 Trade and other English farthings. Fine. 24 pieces

430 Louis XIIII. Bronze Medal. Obv., bust; rev., horseman riding at full speed. "Fuso Hostium Equitatu." Proof. Size 26

431 Java, Turkey, India, French, English, German. All ex. fine, a large proportion of them bright. 25 pieces

432 East Indies, China, France, Italy, and Spain. 40 pieces

433 Sweden, Denmark, Greece, etc. Fair. 25 "

434 Portugal, Brazil, etc. Poor. 25 "

435 Miscellaneous Coppers, half-penny size. Fine. 25 "

436 ——— Farthing size, antique, etc., etc.; some spiel-marks and medalets. Fine. 25 pieces

437 ——— Various sizes. Some rare and fine medalets. 15 pieces

438 ——— Mixed and indifferent. 200 "

439 Excavated Coins; mostly antique. Illegible.

440 Antique of Hadrian, first bronze, and fine medalet of Napoleon I. 2 pieces

441 American Cents, nickel and copper, 1857 to 1866. Nearly all uncirculated. 10 pieces

442 ——— From 1862 to 1866. Brilliant. 20 "

443 ——— Two-cents, 1864, '65, '67, '68. Brilliant. 19 "

444 ——— Shinplasters, 1837–'41. Uncirculated. 4 "

445 ——— Others; very fine, with "ships, colonies, and commerce," "Liberia," etc. 10 pieces

Miscellaneous Coins. 105

446 Store Cards, including "Mott's Token," Woodworth's Planing Machine, Moffet's, Willard's and others. Uncirculated.
7 pieces
447 Gibbs' Card. "The Cow," etc. Uncirculated; in this condition, very rare.
448 Store Cards and shinplasters. 25 pieces
449 E. Cogan's Card, 1860. Splendid proof.
450 Randall & Co. (Baltimore). Fruchlwenger cent, and three cents of 1865. Proof. 4 pieces
451 Miscellaneous lot, consisting of cards, shinplasters, and tokens. 22 pieces
452 California Counter, penny-size; City Hall, same size; California and temperance tokens; Clay, Harrison, Scott, Buchanan, McClellan, etc. 16 pieces
453 Abra-Ham-Lin-Coln. Medalets in nickel, brass, and tin. Proof. 3 pieces
454 Tyson & Co., transfer ticket, etc., etc. 10 "
455 Copperheads. Copper and brass. All bright; a splendid lot. 30 pieces
456 ―――― Another lot. 28 "
457 Silver set of Victoria's Coins, from sixpence to penny. Fine proofs. 5 pieces
458 ―――― Sixpence, fourpence, and threepence. Fine.
3 pieces
459 ―――― Fourpence, George II. Uncirculated, rare; with sixpence of George IV. 2 pieces
460 ―――― English Threepence, penny and half, and penny.
5 pieces.
461 ―――― Dutch E. I. Co. quarter gulden, and Turkish coin, dime-size. 2 pieces
462 ―――― Anna (Scotch). Five-shilling piece, 1705; rev., thistle. Rare.
463 ―――― Itzebu of Japan. Fine.
464 Base Silver of Austria, 20 krs., of France, 1, 1822. Fine.
465 ―――― Danish-American, 1767. 2 pieces
466 ―――― Various denominations and nationalities. 25 "

MISCELLANEOUS ARTICLES.

467 GOLD BROOCH (solid and heavy 18 karat); with onyx cameo stone, black head. Size of stone, 1 inch.
468 SCARF PIN. Onyx and carnelian links united by gold.
469 BRACELET. Double gilt, with handsome agate-onyx stones.
470 DIAMOND RING. Three rose-stones in enameled 18-karat gold.
471 HINDOO Sacrificial Cup. Hammered metal, gilt. Fine and rare.
472 BRONZE Cup on stand. A choice ash-receiver, although not designed for that use. Fine.
473 DRESSED figure of a peasant, *Ex voto*, from a chapel in Italy. Height about 15 inches.
474 ——— Madonna. Very fine and rare.
475 COLLECTION of Political and Military Buttons,—Union and Confederate, "Log Cabin," Sanitary Commission, etc., etc. In very fine order and rare.   62 pieces
476 INDIAN POTTERY. Fragments of terra cotta or earthen, from Western mounds. Very rare.
477 MINERALS. A small collection; with fine and characteristic specimens of Magnesite, Marmolite, Kerolite, Nemelite, Pectolite, Byssolite, Selenite, Kyanite, Amianthus, Staurotide, Copper, Red Oxide of Zinc, Epidote, Garnets, Talc, etc., etc. Sold as one lot.
478 PRIME (W. C.) "Coins, Medals, and Seals—Ancient and Modern. Illustrated," etc. Small quarto, cloth. Fine, clean copy. Rare.
479 COIN CATALOGUES. A very fine lot; many of them scarce, and some *rare*.   30 pieces
480 PAMPHLETS, Magazines, etc.   20 "

www.ingramcontent.com/pod-product-compliance
Lightning Source LLC
Chambersburg PA
CBHW022145160426
43197CB00009B/1438